LIFE LAUNCH

LIFE LAUNCH

A ROADMAP TO AN
EXTRAORDINARY ADULTHOOD

JESSE GIUNTA RAFEH

LIONCREST
PUBLISHING

LIFE LAUNCH
A Roadmap to an Extraordinary Adulthood

ISBN   978-1-5445-0883-2 *Hardcover*
        978-1-5445-0882-5 *Paperback*
        978-1-5445-0881-8 *Ebook*
        978-1-5445-0884-9 *Audiobook*

FOR TONI,
WHO LAUNCHED ME INTO MY OWN ADULTHOOD

CONTENTS

INTRODUCTION

HOW TO CREATE THE LIFE YOU WANT

"The last of human freedoms is to choose one's attitude in a given set of circumstances."

—VIKTOR FRANKL

I met Chloe when she was eighteen years old. Her mother had just kicked her out of the house, and she was spending most of her time drinking and partying. She had no desire to go to college. In fact, she didn't have a clue about what she wanted to do with her life. Meanwhile, she was also struggling in the dating world; she went from casual sex that left her feeling empty to clinging to her romantic partners, who eventually pushed her away.

Chloe came to my office for therapy because she felt lost and wanted to find ways to cope with her emotions. Though her mom had kicked her out of the house, she was still on her parents' health insurance plan, which covered our sessions together.

After a few sessions, it was clear that she wanted to learn how to take care of herself and find a sense of direction. She wanted to know how to connect with people and create healthy relationships, romantic and otherwise. The more we talked, the more Chloe realized that she wanted something more from her life. She knew she was capable of creating a better future for herself, but besides coming to therapy, she had no idea where to start.

Chloe had arrived at that critical transition point between childhood and adulthood. Like so many young adults in the twenty-first century, she was as disoriented as she was overwhelmed. Suddenly, after years of following a prescribed path, she was responsible for making all of the decisions about her life and her future.

It was a pivotal time for her, as it is for all young adults.

THE CHALLENGE OF ADULTHOOD

When you're making the transition from childhood to adulthood, you're setting the stage to create the life you want. But if, like Chloe, you're confused, depressed, or anxious, the transition can feel more overwhelming than amazing. If you're constantly feeling unhappy, how can you know what you really want? If you don't love and accept yourself, how can you create healthy relationships with other people?

On one hand, this is an exciting time. After all, this is the moment when you have the power to decide whether you want to continue being the person you've been up until now. Your world is as close to a blank canvas as it will ever be.

Standing face to face with that blank canvas, however, can be terrifying.

As you begin your transition into adulthood—or even as you're right in the middle of it—you might be wondering, "How do *I* go from feeling stuck to finding happiness? How do I figure out what I want? How do I create strong relationships?"

The truth is that we have to look backward before we can look to the future.

As a kid, everyone made your life decisions for you. You reacted to what happened, but it was your parents'/caregivers' job to create an environment that helped you see the world as a secure, happy, exciting place. You learned to be happy, sad, angry, or scared based on what happened to you as you grew up.

When you transition into adulthood, you're making your own decisions. More often than not, you start from the perspective you learned in childhood—from your parents/caregivers, your friends, and your culture. However, you have the power to adopt a different perspective.

This is one of the most exciting parts of becoming an adult: *You* can choose how you interpret the events in your life.

YOU CREATE YOUR EMOTIONS

I've written this book to share everything I learned, and everything I wish I had known, as I was struggling through my transition into adulthood. I'm also going to share stories and lessons from the young adults I've worked with in the psychotherapy practice I started in 2005.

When we start working together, one of the first things I tell my clients is something a great teacher taught me: "What you resist will persist. And what you accept will transform."

To be human, it's important to let yourself feel the feelings that come up for you. If you don't feel your feelings in their pure form, they build up over time, transforming into defensive emotions like anxiety, anger, depression, or loneliness.

Learning to let go of your defenses and let yourself experience your feelings is the first step to transforming them. We'll focus on ways to do this in chapters 1 through 3 of this book.

Besides allowing yourself to feel, another key to transforming your perspective is to understand is that you can actually influence your own happiness.

As kids, we learn to wait for certain things to happen in order to feel fulfilled. We prolong our happiness based on some external factor we can't control, like taking a trip, staying up late to watch our favorite TV show, or having an ice cream.

As adults, we often adopt the same pattern we had as children. We connect our happiness to external things like having X amount of money, a prestigious job, and/or the perfect partner. "Once I get Y, I'll be happy," you tell yourself. Does that sound familiar?

The truth is, that pattern no longer serves us in adulthood. If we base our happiness on waiting for one specific thing to happen, we actually prevent ourselves from feeling fulfilled.

You can be successful in multiple areas of your life and still be unhappy. Why? It all comes down to how you interpret things. Your relationship to how you view things generates your emotion. In other words, emotions don't happen to you. You create them.

Ultimately, you have the ability to change your relationship with your emotions. Sounds easy, right? It's not. It goes against human instinct. It's a decision you have to make over and over again. This book will give you the tools to understand that the way you feel about the world is up to you. Once you can grasp that idea, it's much easier to get clear about and move toward what you want in your life.

I've seen it happen again and again with my clients, including Chloe. Things didn't automatically get better for her once she realized she could create her own happiness, but they definitely started to shift. She went from drinking and partying to distract herself from her pain to eating vegan, working out regularly, and discovering her passion for product design. After landing a competitive job at a growing startup, she moved to Rome to go to college.

Once she felt better in her body and found a sense of direction, Chloe's relationships started to improve. Little by little, instead of being subjected to the whims of selfish guys and flaky friends, she discovered she had the ability to choose people who met her needs. By taking baby steps, she moved closer to creating healthy relationships for the first time in her life.

I can relate strongly with this aspect of Chloe's story, because I also had to learn to create my own happiness.

MY STORY

I'm the only child of parents who graduated from Stanford University. As I grew up, to say that the pressure to succeed was immense would be an understatement.

For a while, that pressure worked in my favor. I got good grades. I had a bunch of friends. I was on student council.

It all fell apart when I got to high school. My cousin Jason, who was like a brother to me, committed suicide. Two years later, his father killed himself. A year after that, my grandpa, whom I was very close to, died. Meanwhile, my two other cousins were in and out of psych wards; they eventually committed suicide, too.

All at once, young adulthood became a terrifying time for me. I thought: "Well, everyone else is losing their minds and committing suicide. That's probably what's going to happen to me."

I was heading down a bleak path, grieving for my family, and struggling to make sense of my life. Not only did I feel immense sadness, but I also lost all motivation to do anything for myself or anyone else. My grades dropped. I isolated myself from my friends. I developed severe panic attacks and chronic anxiety. I dragged myself through life in survival mode.

My parents were worried about me, so they sent me to therapy. Unfortunately, my first therapist didn't know what to do with me. I was desperate for her to understand how dark and hopeless I felt. But when I shared my feelings with her, the look on her face seemed more disconnected than empathetic.

No matter what I said at the end of a session—whether it was "I'm going to the pumpkin patch after this" or "I hate this life, and I can't go on"—she would always say, "Our time is coming to a close." I left every session with her feeling more alone than ever.

Over the next two years, I felt more depressed and isolated. I teetered between feeling overwhelmed with grief and feeling completely numb. I wanted to cry, but no matter how hard I tried, the tears wouldn't come. So I started cutting myself, just to be able to feel something. That's when the therapist suggested I go to a psych hospital. I felt resigned. After all, this was what my cousins had done. On some level, it made me feel closer to them.

At the psych ward, the doctors diagnosed me with bipolar disorder, which I don't have. They overmedicated me, giving me powerful drugs that made me look and feel crazed. On top of that, I was spending every day with a group of people who were also in a very dark place.

Meanwhile, the drugs made me seem happy on the surface. After five weeks, the doctors released me from the psych ward. Though I was still taking medication, it didn't take long before I sank even deeper into depression. My parents were as concerned about me as they were unhappy with my treatment. As a last resort, they took me to see a different therapist. This was when I met Toni.

I noticed something different about her right away. She looked me in the eye in a way that made me feel like she held hope for me. She brought my parents into the room. She had me sit right next to her. Then she turned to me and said, "Jesse, what do you think this family needs to help you change your life?" Her question overwhelmed me at first. After thinking about it for a minute, I looked at my parents. "I want you to have faith in the fact that I'll be okay," I said. "And I need you to believe that I'm different from my cousins."

BABY STEPS

Thanks to Toni, and to other teachers who mentored me through my teens and twenties, I learned healthy ways to cope with the challenges in my life.

At first, I wanted to tackle everything at once. When I decided to take better care of my body, for example, I thought, "I have to get rid of the cigarettes and the Diet Coke and work out five days a week."

Right away, the negative voice in my mind kicked in. "Why bother?" the voice said, "You're never going to get in shape anyway. And wouldn't it feel better just to stay home and watch a movie?"

Eventually, I recognized where that negative voice was

coming from. It was rooted in my survival instinct, or my ego—and it wanted me to stay right where I was.

Over time, I understood that my negative mind's goals (staying alive) were different from my true self goals (happiness and fulfillment). As long as I kept listening to the negative voice in my head, I was setting myself up to fail. We'll examine this idea in more detail in chapters 1, 3, and 4.

In the meantime, I realized that if I was going to get anywhere, I couldn't tackle everything at once. Instead, I had to take baby steps toward my goals. So I thought about the easiest way to get myself moving, and I gently talked myself through it. Taking a five-minute walk or going a week without Diet Coke may not sound like a big deal. But each step represented a choice to move myself in a positive direction—and that meant something.

Over time, as I learned to celebrate after every baby step, I created a positive momentum loop that motivated me to keep moving forward. I also started to find joy in my life's possibilities. We'll explore the concept of rewarding yourself, along with the idea of taking baby steps, in almost every chapter of the book, particularly in chapters 1, 3, 4, and 5.

Ultimately, through a combination of psychotherapy, spiritual practice, and taking care of my physical body, I learned to fall in love with myself. I went from being in a dark, exhausted place—where it took every ounce of energy I had to survive each day—to understanding how to create my own happiness and fulfillment.

I also redefined my relationships with my parents. Instead

of feeling angry about their imperfections, I grew to understand that my parents' emotionally stunted childhoods sometimes made it hard for them to let me fully express my feelings. In the meantime, I cultivated a group of lifelong friends. Eventually, as I learned to connect more deeply with my true self, I met the love of my life.

FROM THERAPY TO THERAPIST

As I worked through my feelings of anxiety and depression with Toni, I grew to love the process of therapy. Besides teaching me to release the emotions I was holding on to, she taught me about psychological theory and the ideas of fulfillment and happiness. With her help, I developed the coping skills to heal myself and find happiness. She also introduced me to my life goal: to become a successful psychotherapist in private practice, focusing on young adults.

I went straight through college to graduate school. I was the youngest person in my class. On top of that, I was socially awkward, and I didn't have great fashion sense. I spent my free time watching *Gilmore Girls* reruns and snowboarding. I hadn't ever been in a serious romantic relationship.

None of my classmates took me seriously at first. The feeling I got from them on the first day of classes was: "Isn't it cute that this girl dreams of becoming a therapist? She thinks she can help others because she was sad. Awww..."

The condescending looks on my classmates' faces, not to mention the way they talked down to me during our initial role-plays, mirrored my greatest fears: that I was too young, not to mention too naïve, to think I could actually help people or start a business. However, instead of feeding my anxiety, my classmates helped me move past it. I'd always loved being the underdog. I liked surprising people who underestimated me. I was determined to prove them wrong. So I did.

I opened my private therapy practice at twenty-four. Most of my first clients were young people who looked at me and saw someone they could relate to. I helped them develop an understanding of themselves and the adults in their lives. I also helped parents empathize with their teens. I became a bridge between two generations of people.

Since then, I've helped hundreds of young adults successfully transition into their lives and get in touch with their true selves. This book is their story, too.

WHY I BELIEVE IN MERGING PSYCHOLOGY AND SPIRITUALITY[1]

As I was trying to find my way out of anxiety and depression, I had an important realization: if I truly wanted to transform my life, I had to work both the psychological and the spiritual side.

Psychology helped me get in touch with my negative emo-

---

1   I recognize that the words "spiritual" and "spirituality" can be a turn-off. In this book, I'm not
    referring to spirituality in a religious sense (though if religion is a source of comfort and helps
    you see the big picture, I encourage you to explore it). Instead, I use the words "spiritual" and
    "spirituality" to describe the idea of having a big-picture philosophy that helps you find calm—
    whatever that philosophy happens to be. To put it another way, integrating a spiritual perspective
    is about understanding the difference between the larger, universal picture and the smaller,
    individual picture of your life—and there are lots of different ways to arrive at this perspective.

tions and release them once I figured out where they were coming from.

Meanwhile, spirituality—which is the term I use for being able to see the big picture—helped me free myself from negative emotions without dissecting them.

Initially, I dealt with anxiety and depression by scrutinizing each of my negative thoughts and tying it back to a childhood experience. I turned to psychology and psychotherapy, which gave me a system to strip all of my experiences down to their core, find the roots of my fear, and release responsibility for my trauma.

In other words, psychology helped me develop an awareness of my past to see how it was affecting my present. After years of applying and studying psychological theories, I became a fairly happy, high-functioning person. But I could still feel anxiety below the surface.

Though I'd spent years resisting anything to do with spirituality, I decided to go a meditation retreat. At first, I couldn't find words to describe what was happening inside me. It was pure bliss: suddenly I was so overwhelmed by the beauty of the world, by the trees, by the people around me, that I started to cry.

I was totally confused. Up to that point, I'd thought of myself as an analytical person. I was proud of living in my head. I liked to overthink things. Until that retreat, I had no idea how powerful it could be to let go of what was in my mind.

For the first time, I realized that I didn't have to dissect every negative aspect of my life. Just recognizing the negative was a way to free myself from it, if only for a moment. Why? For the first time, I realized that negative thoughts were part of everyone's experience of being human. Understanding that my negative mind was rooted in my natural survival instincts helped me see that there was nothing "wrong" with me.

After that retreat, I understood the power of integrating psychology and spirituality in terms of learning to cope with the full spectrum of our emotions. To cope with our pain, we need to explore both sides. If we only work the spiritual side, we could end up in denial because it's difficult to release all of our negative emotions and past traumas that way. If we just focus on psychology, all the negative thoughts and feelings that arise can bog us down.

So how do we work both sides? Let's look at an example: Imagine you've been rolling around in the mud. Say someone hoses you off. Most of the dirt may be gone, but there's still mud on your body. To get completely clean, you'll need to scrub off the stubborn spots in the shower. In this example, spirituality, or big picture thinking, is the hose, helping you clean off the surface dirt (i.e., enabling you to see the nature of your negative mind). Psychology is the equivalent of scrubbing off those hard-to-reach spots in the shower, where you address the dirt that's left over (i.e., the doubts and fears that come up over and over again in your mind).

Ultimately, I achieved a certain level of peace and happiness in my life with the help of psychology—but then I hit a ceiling. Spirituality helped me go beyond that ceiling and led me to realize that not everything my mind was telling me was important. By embracing both, I found a way to move more quickly—and more gracefully—through my negative emotional experiences.

That's the approach I take with all my clients, and I've translated that approach into this book.

WHY THIS BOOK IS FOR YOUNG ADULTS

Though they come to me for different reasons, what my clients have in common is that they're facing a very pivotal time in their lives. That's what I love about working with young adults. As frightening as the transition into adulthood can be, it's also a moment when we're capable of real change.

All three of my cousins went through their breakdowns when they were in their twenties. This is one of the main reasons I work with, and am writing this book for, people who are just launching into adulthood. I want to help you move through your fear and find joy in the possibilities in your life.

However, even if you're deeper into adulthood, and you're looking to transform a particular aspect of your life, you can also learn from the principles and apply the concepts we'll explore in these pages.

HOW TO USE THIS BOOK

This book is a 360-degree guide to what you need to create your extraordinary life. It's a holistic guide to learning how to cope with anxiety, anger, and depression—and how to take care of your spirit. It offers practical guidance for keeping your body in balance, assessing your relationship with alcohol and drugs, finding your professional direction, and reaching your financial goals. It will give you the tools to create and sustain healthy relationships with your parents/caregivers, your friends, and your romantic partners.

This book is designed to meet you where you are. You can choose to read it from start to finish. You can also skip ahead to the chapter on attracting a romantic partner, or skip back to the chapter on anxiety, or to any of the chapters that explore a facet of your life you want to address right now. It's entirely up to you.

I've organized this book the way I approach my work with clients, starting with your spirit and your emotions in Part I. In chapters 1 through 3, we'll look at how to cope with anxiety, anger, and depression from both a psychological and a spiritual perspective. In chapter 4, "How to Take Care of Your Spirit," we'll explore ways to help you find your calm and separate yourself from the survival voice in your head. (If you're not a meditator, don't worry! We'll also discuss other ways to change your relationship with your emotions.)

Once you learn about ways to cope with the emotional challenges you're facing, we move on to Part II, the mind/body section of the book. We'll look at specific aspects of your life you may want to transform: your body and health, your relationship with alcohol and drugs, your career, and your finances.

In Parts I and II, the goal is to help you create a healthy relationship with yourself. The more you can accept and love yourself, the easier it is to create healthy relationships in your life. In other words, before you can fall in love with someone else, you have to learn to fall in love with yourself. This is our focus in Part III, where we'll explore how to realign your relationship with your parents/caregivers, create healthy friendships, attract the right partner, and sustain a healthy romantic relationship.

I want you to do more than read this book. My hope is that it supports and inspires you to do things right now to make yourself feel better. I've designed the practices at the end of each chapter with that hope in mind.

If you're doing the practices—as I'd ask a client to do between sessions—you're deepening your understanding of ideas that might be hard to grasp if you just read them on the page. They're designed to help you build your coping mechanisms on the way to becoming the best version of yourself.

To make the most of these practices, I suggest you buy a journal or start a journal in your phone; the act of writing things down helps you process your thoughts and track your progress as you grow.

IT'S UNCOMFORTABLE TO GROW—BUT IT'S WORTH IT

Before you get started on this journey, there's something I'd like you to know: it's uncomfortable to grow. Making changes in your life might not actually feel good at first, but that doesn't mean you should give up.

We live in a culture where we tell ourselves, "I want to feel good, and I want to feel good right now." Feeling good right now doesn't always lead to your long-term happiness, though. And it's your long-term happiness that we're after.

As a therapist, I hold the hope that you can move through whatever challenges you're having in your life right now and create a positive future for yourself. While you read this book, you're hearing what I would say to you if I were your therapist.

You have the ability to create whatever you want in your life: excitement, fulfillment, peace, fun, growth, love. Any experience you want, whether it's at your job, whether you want to travel, whether it's finding love you want, is possible for you. The world is your blank canvas. This is what I believe. After you read this book, I hope you believe it, too.

PART I

EMOTIONS AND SPIRIT

CHAPTER 1

HOW TO COPE WITH ANXIETY

At nineteen years old, my client Diego had hit bottom. He was failing out of junior college. He didn't have a job. His girlfriend had broken up with him. Little by little, his group of friends was dissolving. By the time I met him, the idea of leaving his house made him feel so anxious he would get nauseous.

The more time he spent alone, the harder it was for Diego to go out. He avoided parties. He did everything he could to keep from going out.

After months of working through his feelings of anxiety, he was ready to take his first baby step: going to a meditation meet-up, where he wouldn't have to talk. Still, the idea of interacting with the people at the meet-up scared him. "What if I can't do it?" he said. "What if the people don't like me?"

On the day of the meet-up, he felt sick to his stomach. When he got in the car, the nausea got worse. The closer he drove to the meditation studio, the louder the voices in his head became: "This is so stupid," he thought. "Why am I so freaked out? There's nothing to be afraid of!"

Those self-judgments were the building blocks of his anxiety.

WHAT IS ANXIETY AND WHERE DOES IT COME FROM?

Anxiety is the fear of your fear. More precisely, it's the effect of being stuck in your fear and trying to keep it at bay.

Anxiety is also the most common mental health problem in the United States. Why? In this culture, and sometimes in our families, we learn to suppress our fear. When we get scared about something—whether it's being able to pay our bills, get on an airplane, or make a phone call to follow up on a job application—we tell ourselves it's not okay to feel our fear. We're taught to see it as a weakness. Then we try to talk ourselves out of it. Unfortunately, this only increases our feelings of anxiety.

But where does all this fear come from in the first place?

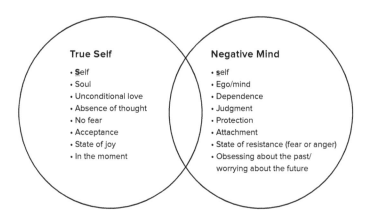

True Self
- **S**elf
- Soul
- Unconditional love
- Absence of thought
- No fear
- Acceptance
- State of joy
- In the moment

Negative Mind
- self
- Ego/mind
- Dependence
- Judgment
- Protection
- Attachment
- State of resistance (fear or anger)
- Obsessing about the past/ worrying about the future

As the graphic on this page shows, we all have two selves. The first is our true self. This is the part of us that feels unconditional love and acceptance. Our true self is in the moment. It's the best version of who we are.

Our second self is the negative mind, which shows up in the form of feelings like anxiety and self-protection.

If your thoughts are making you anxious, if you're obsessing about the past or worrying about the future, it's your negative mind talking. On the other hand, if you're savoring the moment, feeling happy, at peace, and connecting to the world around you, you're in your true self.

Throughout the day, you experience aspects of both your negative mind and your true self. As the graphic shows, you're often functioning in both at the same time. However, if you suffer from anxiety, it can feel like your negative mind is doing most of the talking, eclipsing your true self. Why does this happen?

The negative mind, also known as the ego, is the psychological expression of our survival instinct. Even though most of us no longer have to worry about day-to-day survival, our negative mind still functions as if we live in the jungle. It hasn't caught up to our twenty-first-century reality, where most of our basic survival needs are met. In other words, *our minds haven't evolved to match our circumstances.*

Most of the time, what the negative mind is telling us doesn't correspond with our present reality. If you're reading this book, I'm hoping you don't need to be thinking about life and death on a daily basis. I'm assuming you have shelter and enough food to eat.

Your negative mind doesn't know that, though. Once you've taken care of your basic needs, the negative mind automatically fills that empty space in your head with worries, concerns, and whatever it thinks you need to stay alive.

Your negative mind has no desire to make you happy. It's not there to bring you inner peace. Its one and only job is to keep you alive, and the best way to do that is to keep you in a hyper-vigilant state where you're assessing danger all the time. According to the negative mind, if you're too calm, you might not notice the tiger creeping up behind you, or the threat of being kicked out of your tribe.

In other words, the negative mind is always searching for the thought or emotion that's going to trigger your survival instincts. All too often, that emotion is anxiety.

The key to coping with anxiety is learning to identify, and eventually calm, the negative mind. And the first step in calming the negative mind is to understand that you're not alone in your feelings.

YOU'RE NOT ALONE

One of the keys to moving beyond anxiety is to change the way you think about it. Many people think anxiety is unique to them. However, when my clients refer to their feelings as "my anxiety," I tell them that everyone is anxious to some degree.

When you say, "I have anxiety" or "I'm an anxious person," you're taking ownership of those feelings. When you tell yourself that you're alone in your anxiety, it becomes part of your identity.

Instead of thinking of it as part of your identity, it helps to look at anxiety as an emotion you're dealing with and learning to cope with. That's when you begin to change your relationship with it.

For example, I was painfully shy growing up. My parents were constantly worrying about my lack of confidence, and about the fact that it was hard for me to look people in the eye and introduce myself. Over time, I interpreted my parents' desire for me to be more confident as a personal failing. As a result, my shyness escalated into a fear of meeting new people. I started to think of myself as an anxious person. "My anxiety" was part of who I was.

However, once I learned to accept that it was natural to feel anxious in a social setting—and noticed that I wasn't the only one at parties who felt nervous—I stopped seeing

anxiety as a weakness that was unique to me. As an introvert, I just needed some time to open up to people. Instead
of judging that shy part of myself, I learned to organically enter social situations as I was ready—and connect
with people in a meaningful way. I went from thinking of
myself as an anxious person to recognizing, and honoring,
my sensitivity.

As I told myself then, and as I tell my clients now, anxiety is
not something that's wrong with you. It's a sign that something isn't functioning correctly in our emotional system
(i.e., it's a maladaptive coping mechanism). Ultimately, it's
something we're all facing in one way or another. Once we
understand that we're not alone in feeling anxious, we can
start to let those feelings go.

So what else can you do to cope with anxiety? Well, as it
turns out, quite a lot.

WHAT CAN YOU DO ABOUT ANXIETY?

It's one thing to think of anxiety as a maladaptive coping
mechanism. It's another to cope with it when it comes up
for you. Let's work through an example of making a phone
call to a stranger—something that brings up anxious feelings for many of us—to see the specific steps you can take
to move through anxiety in almost any situation.

Here's the scenario: you've been looking for a job for several months. You've emailed dozens of applications to
potential employers, but not one has responded. One of
your friends, who's excellent at landing competitive jobs

and internships, suggests you change your strategy: "You might have to follow up with a phone call," she says.

"Oh, my gosh," you say. "A phone call?"

You're terrified, but you don't want to admit it. You tell yourself it's ridiculous to feel afraid. It's just a stupid phone call, right?

Instead of judging yourself for being afraid, an important first step in changing your relationship with anxiety is to validate your fear. *It's okay to be scared.*

Making a phone call isn't something you do very often nowadays. Before, when you wanted to order a pizza, you had to pick up the phone. When you wanted to buy a piece of furniture, you had to go to a store and talk with a salesperson. These days, you don't have very many opportunities to connect and communicate with other people you don't know. No wonder making a phone call can feel like a big deal. Again, *it's okay to be scared.*

At first, it can be challenging to accept what you fear. You might resist or reject the idea. If it's especially hard for you, ask yourself this: would you talk to your favorite five-year-old the way you talk to yourself? More often than not, the answer is "no."

No matter how many times you have to say it, tell yourself it's okay to be scared—no matter what you're afraid of.

FIGURE OUT WHAT YOU'RE AFRAID OF

Once you get to a place where you can accept your fear, the next step is to figure out the thoughts triggering the anxiety.

Let's return to our phone call. What is it that you're actually afraid of? Think it through for a moment. In this situation, my clients usually say, "There are no thoughts. I'm just really anxious."

Sometimes it's hard to pinpoint these thoughts because you've had to ignore them or deny them for a while. Give yourself the time and space to figure them out.

Start by making a list of the things that bring up anxiety for you in this scenario. Are you afraid of being annoying? Of bothering someone? Of making a bad impression? Or are you afraid it won't make a difference?

Add any ideas you want to the list. Then read through the ideas one by one. Take your time. Pay attention to how your body reacts to each item on the list. Does your jaw tighten? Does your heart beat faster? Does your stomach clench? Do you feel tingling anywhere?

Once you can figure out what's making you feel afraid, you can start to work through it. You might think it's silly. You might realize it has no basis in reality.

No matter what the fear is, or how silly it seems, it's important to be loving and empathetic about it. Go back to how you would treat your favorite five-year-old, and apply that gentleness to yourself. You're not weak for feeling this way. It's okay—and understandable—to be scared of making a bad impression, catching someone at the wrong time, or not getting the job. Again, you can trace these emotions back to your negative mind, which is trying to protect you by keeping you in a hyper-vigilant state.

After you've zeroed in the source of your fear, say it out loud. Whatever it is. This automatically releases a part of it. Once you articulate your fear, it has less control over you.

COME BACK TO THE PRESENT MOMENT

All anxiety is rooted in thoughts about the future. Our phone call is a classic example: All the fear we've connected to it is based on what we think might happen later on. It has nothing to do with what's happening right now.

Let's imagine you're preparing to pick up the phone. How do you calm yourself down? By bringing yourself back to the present moment. There are a few ways you can do this:

- Concentrate on your breathing. Inhale and exhale into your belly.

- Ask yourself: "Is everything okay in this moment?" Nine times out of ten, it is.

- Do an activity that gives you pleasure and encourages you to focus (e.g., taking a walk, dancing to your favorite song, stretching/yoga, gardening).

- Work out. Moving your body releases endorphins, the so-called happiness hormones that help create a feeling of calm.

- Tighten and loosen your muscles starting from your toes and moving up through your body.

- Meditate. (We'll explore meditation, and the different ways to do it, in chapter 4.)

Feel free to experiment until you figure out which techniques work best for you.

One thing to keep in mind is that the greater your level of anxiety, the simpler the activity should be. For example, if you're having a panic attack, find the position that makes you feel most comfortable (e.g., lying on the floor), and focus on your breathing. Inhale to a count of four, then exhale to a count of eight; the uneven breath count leads you to concentrate harder, which helps calm your nervous system. If lying down isn't an option, you can also kneel in a crouched position and drink a glass of water slowly. This slows down your heart rate and brings your body back to normal. Finally, keep telling yourself, "I will be okay."

FEEL THE FEAR AND DO IT ANYWAY

So you've accepted your fear. You've figured out its source. You've brought yourself back to the present moment. Now you're finally ready to pick up the phone. But, wait—your heart is beating like crazy. Your hands are sweating. You can't believe how nervous you are. You can't bring yourself to start dialing the number.

This is the point where many of my clients get stuck. They think, "I'm going to work through all the anxiety about the phone call, then—and only then—I'll pick up the phone."

It doesn't work that way.

You won't overcome all your feelings of anxiety before you pick up the phone—or before you do anything that scares you.

Instead, your goal is to get to the point where you can do it in spite of your fear. In the end, what helps you release the anxiety is making the phone call and seeing that nothing bad came of it. Maybe you weren't perfect, but you survived.

The more you stop yourself from doing something, the more frightening it becomes. The more you can allow yourself to feel your fear and still do the things that intimidate you, the more trust and courage you build inside yourself, the less anxiety has control over you and your choices.

ACKNOWLEDGE YOURSELF

Any time you do something in spite of feeling anxiety about it, it's important to acknowledge yourself for doing it—no matter how small you think it is.

In the case of our phone call, if you've managed to work through your fear, pick up the phone, and make the call, don't just put the phone down and move on to the next thing on your list. Take a moment to say to yourself, "Hey, Self! You did it! No matter what happens, you gave it your best shot, even though you were afraid. Great job!"

It may feel silly, or even ridiculous, to talk to yourself this way. At first, you might resist doing it. But recognizing yourself every time you take a step forward is a crucial part of coping with anxiety.

Have you ever visited an elementary school classroom? Do you notice that whenever the teacher asks a question, there are a bunch of kids with their hands in the air going, "Oh, oh! Pick me! Pick me!" Why is that? They want the positive reinforcement that comes with having the right answer.

As we grow older, we don't outgrow our need for positive reinforcement. We've just learned to numb ourselves to the idea that we want and need it. As children, we can't give ourselves positive reinforcement. But the beauty of being an adult is that we can if we practice.

When you reward yourself every time you do something that makes you feel anxious, you interrupt the negative thought patterns that lead to feelings of anxiety. Instead of letting your fear control you, you build your motivation to keep doing the things that scare you. Not only that, you gradually develop the strength to take on bigger challenges.

EMDR

If you feel like you've tried everything and are still stuck in anxiety, or if you're looking for additional ways to ease anxiety, Eye Movement Desensitization and Reprocessing (EMDR) therapy might be an option for you. EMDR is a form of therapy that helps people process trauma by connecting both hemispheres of the brain through rapid eye movements, alternating sounds, or body tapping.

The general idea behind EMDR is that when we're traumatized (i.e., when we've experienced big emotions), we store these experiences on the right side of the brain. However, when we try to process these experiences later on, we mostly access them through talking, using the left side of the brain.

The theory behind EMDR is that if you connect the right and left sides of the brain while processing big emotions, you can release what's been stuck. As I mentioned in the introduction, emotions are temporary, so EMDR represents another way to allow them to move through us.

Though it's not a quick fix, EMDR can be a starting point, or a helpful stop on your journey toward happiness and fulfillment. Another bonus? You can even learn to perform EMDR therapy on yourself. See the Appendix for more information and resources.

BIG PICTURE STRATEGIES FOR COPING WITH ANXIETY

Ultimately, there are two ways to ease anxiety. The first way is to address the anxious loop directly, from a psychological perspective, as in the phone call example above. The second way is to take a big-picture (or "spiritual") approach. Both are equally effective and important to practice.

The big-picture approach to easing anxiety involves interrupting your mind's natural tendency to shift into survival mode. "Thank you, mind, but that's enough," you can tell yourself. "I'm going to take a break from you now." Doing things like taking a walk or watching a television show—or whatever activity helps you calm down—helps lower the volume on the negative voice in your head. The idea is that you don't have to "solve" your feelings of anxiety right now.

Sometimes when we're anxious, it can feel like a canker sore. We run our tongues over it again and again, but the sore doesn't heal. If you're feeling like you just can't deal with your fear, and you're not in the space to figure out where it's coming from, give yourself permission to take a break. Do something that brings out your feelings of calm, peace, and fulfillment. You can always return to investigate the roots of your fear later.

Taking a break from anxiety doesn't mean you're in denial about what you're feeling, or that you're not healing. In fact, it's *just as important* to step back from your emotions when they feel overwhelming as it is to do the psychological work around them. In the end, both processes will help you grow.

REPLACE THE EMPTY SPACE IN YOUR MIND WITH MEANING

Again, if you're reading this book, I'm assuming you're able to meet your basic needs for food and shelter. What that means, as I mentioned in the first part of this chapter, is that your negative mind, which is rooted in your survival instinct, basically has nothing to do. So it's looking for something latch onto, and it fills the space in your head with worries and anxiety.

Having too much empty, unstructured time in your life, on

top of not having a goal or a direction, is very challenging for the human psyche. It can often lead to anxiety and/
or depression.

Once your basic needs are met, what can you do to quiet
your negative mind and all the anxiousness it stirs up? Fill
the space in your mind with things that have meaning.
What are your goals? What are your dreams? It doesn't
matter what they are, but if you want to change your relationship with anxiety over the long-term, it's important to
find a direction.

We'll look more at how to find direction in your life in chapter 5. For now, think about finding a place to put your energy
that feels empowering and fulfilling to you. It doesn't have
to be a professional goal. It could be an art piece. It could
be charity work. It could be taking care of your family. The
important thing is that it's challenging you in some way. If
it's not pushing you to grow, learn something new, or evolve
somehow, you're giving your negative mind the space to
take over.

A SPECK OR PART OF A WHOLE

Another technique for calming anxiety is to shift your perspective. If you're the kind of person who thinks everything
you do is important, and that there's an imaginary audience
scrutinizing all your activities, understanding that the world
actually doesn't depend on your existence can be a calming
thought. To put it another way, if you're a high-achieving,
type-A perfectionist, it can be helpful to remind yourself
that you're just a speck in the universe. If what you're worried about doesn't matter in the larger scheme of things, it

takes the pressure off. It also frees you to go about creating your own internal happiness.

In those moments when I'm taking on the weight of the world, and thinking my clients won't be able to cope if I'm sick, it helps to remind myself that my existence doesn't really matter. The idea that people will adapt and carry on if I can't go to work that day is a source of comfort.

For some of us, however, the idea that we're just a speck in the universe isn't comforting. If we feel like we're alone, we don't matter, or what we do can't possibly make a difference in the world, we need a different perspective. If these are the feelings feeding your anxiety, it sometimes helps to experiment with the idea that you're part of a larger whole.

In other words, think of yourself as a part of a system where what you do affects not only you but a greater magnitude of people. This is what's known as the butterfly effect, where a small change can cause bigger changes to happen.

This idea was very empowering for Diego, whose story starts this chapter. When he became conscious of who he was and thought about the impact he could have through his connection with the wider world, it helped him move through his fear.

After that first meditation meet-up, Diego gradually re-entered the world. He started going to the meditation meet-up every week. He joined a yoga class. He taught himself how to cook, making healthy meals for his family, which took the pressure off his mom to do the cooking. Thanks to Diego, his mom had more energy to focus on her own needs, which made her feel happier and more fulfilled.

Diego also attended meditation retreats, where he connected with people in a meaningful way. Over time, as he worked up the courage to share his experiences with meditation, he began to inspire other young people to start meditating. As he continued to make small changes in his own life, Diego not only started to feel better himself; he also noticed how his actions created a ripple effect and had a positive impact on other people, too.

Instead of feeling like his emotions were happening to him, Diego eventually realized that he actually had power over them. Over time, he understood that he could choose the feelings he wanted to hold onto, along with the ones he wanted to let go of. This was the last important step for him in learning to cope with anxiety.

It's also one of the keys to dealing with anger, which is the topic of chapter 2.

PRACTICE

Take a week and make a note every time you get anxious. (Use your phone for these notes or write them down in a journal.)

Note what you were thinking and what happened right before these feelings came up.

At the end of the week, review your notes. See if you can identify the specific thoughts or themes that trigger your anxiety. For example, "Oh, I felt anxious eleven times this week. It was when I was worried about the time and scared about being late."

Choose one triggering thought or theme that keeps coming up for you. Then ask yourself these three questions, and write down the answers:

What are the judgments you have about yourself around this specific trigger? For example: "It's so stupid that I'm feeling anxious right now," or "Why can't I be like everyone else and just get on the plane?"

What do you think your root fears are? (Our fears are often connected to an emotional injury in childhood. They can also be connected to survival-related fears, like getting kicked out of our tribe, being in physical danger, not having enough resources to meet our basic needs, or perceiving that someone we care about might be in danger.)

What can you say to yourself in order to calm this fear? If you feel anxiety around being unlikeable, for example, you can tell yourself something like: "I'm a likable person with good intentions. The people that matter to me will see that."

In other situations, it helps to think about the worst-case scenario. For example, "I'm not going to end up homeless and starving," or "Statistically speaking, the plane is unlikely to crash."

In most cases, it also helps to come back to the present moment: inhale to a count of four and exhale to a count of eight. Then ask your-self what's happening right now. You can also tell yourself something along the lines of, "I survived all my moments of anxiousness in the past, and I'll survive this one, too."

Now take a week and use the calming phrases you created every time your fear comes up. In your phone or in a journal, note how your calming words/thoughts are affecting you. Do they relieve any of your feelings of anxiety? If so, keep coming back to your calming thoughts when your fear comes up. If not, reevaluate what you're saying to yourself until you land on something that helps ease your fear.

CHAPTER 2

HOW TO DEAL WITH ANGER

When my client Joley walked into my office one beautiful summer day, I could see she was upset. Her jaw was tense. She had her arms crossed tightly over her chest. There were dark circles under her eyes, as if she'd hardly slept.

Her voice shook as she told me what was happening. A few days earlier, her best friend Erin had made a comment on social media that really bothered Joley. She showed me the post on her phone: "There's all this pressure to speak carefully now," Erin had written. "One wrong word and you're a racist."

Erin is white. Joley is half Filipino. At twenty-one, Joley was starting to realize how growing up in a white-dominated world had affected her. Instead of acknowledging her identity, she'd learned to suppress it—until now. Now she was developing her awareness around being a woman of color. For the first time in her life, she was verbalizing her experience.

When Erin made that comment on social media, Joley's first reaction was anger. But she didn't feel comfortable expressing it. "It's no big deal," she told me. "And if I try to explain it to her, she won't get it. No white person can get it."

Joley had no desire to bring up the issue. She wanted to move on and pretend she hadn't seen Erin's post.

I pushed back. Instead of resisting the anger, or setting it aside, I suggested we look for a way to communicate it to Erin.

"How can we do that?" Joley said.

The first step was to deconstruct the anger.

ANGER IS A SECONDARY EMOTION

Though we have four basic feelings—mad, glad, sad, and scared—anger is actually a secondary emotion, a defense against fear and sadness.

Anger is different from other emotions: you can listen to it, you can express it, you can do whatever you want with it, but the only way to make it go away is to figure out the vulnerability underneath it.

If you come across a dog in a corner and it growls, it's not mad at you. It's growling because it's scared. It wants to protect itself. Our human anger works the same way. It's an instinctive response to prevent others from seeing that you're feeling weak, scared, or vulnerable.

Fear is the most common emotion at the root of anger,

though sometimes there's sadness mixed in as well. So the name of the game for deconstructing anger is to find the fear. What are you actually afraid of?

When Erin made that comment on social media, Joley's immediate response was anger. But what was at the bottom of her anger? Joley was afraid that Erin didn't understand her experience. Erin was her best friend. If they weren't on the same page, how could they continue to be close?

CONFUSING ANGER WITH ASSERTIVENESS

Joley had learned to swallow her feelings in childhood. When she turned thirteen, though, she started to express her own opinions. One day, she told her father she thought he was old-fashioned and anti-feminist. They had a huge argument. Not long after that, he left for the Philippines and barely spoke to her for a year.

What did this experience teach her? If she expressed herself, people would abandon her. She would be isolated. She wouldn't get her basic needs met. When we look at Joley's emotional history, it's not hard to understand why she was so reluctant to bring up her reaction to Erin's comment on social media. We'll go into more depth about how your emotional patterns from childhood impact you in adulthood in chapter 9.

In the meantime, I also have clients whose experience is very different from Joley's. They have no problem expressing their feelings and speaking up when they're angry. On one hand, it's great that they have the ability to voice what they're feeling.

On the other hand, sometimes they confuse anger with assertiveness.[2] They think their anger makes them powerful. By walking around ready for a fight, they think they're commanding respect or claiming their space.

For example, my client Leo used to have horrible arguments with his mom, who can't see things from anyone else's perspective. Eventually, his mom kicked him out of the house when Leo was eighteen, and he had to figure out how to support himself on his own. For a few years, he was too angry with his mother to have a relationship with her.

Eventually, after he learned to take care of himself and develop a clear plan for his future, Leo felt ready to reconnect with his mother. Before he could do that, though, he had to go underneath his anger and figure out what he was afraid of. He had to evaluate his own role in the conflict, even if his mother wasn't willing to do the same.

At first, Leo thought that approach sounded weak. "I want my mom to treat me with respect," he said. "I don't want her to walk all over me."

Leo's fear was that his mother was attacking him; he felt like his mom was out to get him. But the reality was his mother was just being his mother. She'd been through her own traumas. Her anger was actually a defense to push people away emotionally so they couldn't hurt her.

After he tapped into the fear beneath his anger, Leo could see things more clearly from his mother's perspective.

---

2 True assertiveness is expressing your feelings without judgment or anger.

Over time, he accepted that anger was a weak place for him to live.

By figuring out his vulnerabilities and communicating what he truly felt, he started tapping into his emotional power. Even when his mother responded to him with anger or judgment, Leo didn't hide behind an angry mask. He learned to see those reactions as part of his mother's story. Meanwhile, Leo was writing his own.

EXPRESSING ANGER VIA JUDGMENT

While outrage or indignation can be ways of expressing anger and directing it outward, judgment is the intellectualization of anger. If you're in a situation where you don't feel powerful, judgment is a calmer alternative. It's anger without the heightened senses, the shaking, the fast-beating heart, and the adrenaline. It's a way to devalue other people and make yourself feel better in the process.

Let's return to the example with Leo's mother. Sometimes she's able to express her love for her son. Other times, she lashes out in judgment, telling Leo he's a horrible son who's manipulative and selfish, who just wants people for their money, and who doesn't take care of his mother.

Like many people, when she feels insecure or scared, Leo's mom turns to judgment. It's a way for her to gain fake power. If she wanted to gain real power, she'd have to address what she was feeling insecure about, instead of temporarily soothing herself by making Leo feel small.

If you frequently catch yourself judging other people, try

this experiment: See how long you can go without talking negatively about them. When you observe yourself thinking in a judgmental way, focus on your own feelings. Then shift your focus to the emotions of the other person. When you shift your perspective this way, you de-intellectualize your anger, and your communication becomes honest and powerful. Something like, "My mom annoys me so much..." becomes "I feel guilty that my mom feels lonely now that I don't live at home anymore."

FIND YOUR FEAR

Whether you tend to swallow your anger or direct it outward, the key to transforming it is to find the fear underneath it. If you're getting angry, it's a warning signal. An interaction has pushed an unresolved button inside you. You're feeling afraid of something. So how do you figure out what it is?

The five most common anger-triggering fears are:

1. **I don't have value.** Example: "My boyfriend/girlfriend doesn't romance me. That means they don't really love me."

2. **I'm misunderstood and alone.** Example: "My friends don't get me." Or "So-and-so isn't texting me back."

3. **I'm not going to get my needs met.** Example: "If I tell my parents/caregivers how I really feel, they'll get angry or defensive."

4. **I can't be a good person and take care of myself.** Example: "My mom makes me feel guilty about not

taking care of her, but if I do what she asks, I don't get what I want. If I don't do what she asks, I feel like an ungrateful daughter/son."

5. **I'm scared someone I care about is not going to be okay (sometimes to the point of death).** Example: "My friend is dating someone who treats her badly."

What do all of these fears have in common? They're rooted in the negative mind's survival instinct, a concept we explored in chapter 1 (and which we'll look at in more detail in chapter 4). Since one of our primary survival-related fears is getting kicked out of our tribe, it can sometimes feel like a life-and-death issue if we're not getting along with others. This is why gaining other people's acceptance feels so important—and why it often triggers anger.

When you're working to find the fear beneath your anger, try to verbalize what your negative mind is telling you—and see how it might connect to a survival-related fear.

Why is it so important to find your fear? If you don't figure out what's making you feel vulnerable, you run the risk of unconsciously creating what you fear. In other words, when you push people away in anger, your fears (e.g., being alone, not having value, or not getting your needs met) become your reality instead of emotions you need to work through.

IT'S NOT ABOUT YOU

Besides finding your fear, another key to unraveling anger is to understand that people aren't out to hurt you. We tend to be so focused on ourselves, and so prone to taking things personally, that we often end up creating stories in our minds about why people treat us in certain ways.

In reality, however, we don't understand the meaning behind other people's behavior—though we think we do. The truth is, we can't know the reasons others act the way they do.

We constantly tell ourselves stories about strangers we meet. What did that flight attendant have against me? Why is the lady at the DMV being so nasty to me? We don't know why. But one thing's for sure: they don't know you. So how could they be angry with *you*?

The easiest way to de-escalate your feelings in these situations is to make an effort to understand things from the other person's perspective. How long has that flight attendant been on duty? Is the lady at the DMV bored out of her mind? Worried about her kids?

We don't just tell ourselves stories about strangers. We do it with the people close to us, too. Since we know them well, it's harder to grasp that we don't know the meaning of their behavior. Why does my brother refuse to talk to me? He thinks I'm a horrible person. Why isn't my girlfriend texting me back? She doesn't love me anymore. Again, it's our negative mind that creates these stories, to keep us in a hyper-vigilant state.

Let's go back to the example of Leo's mother once more. When she says hurtful things like, "You're a horrible son," and, "You're selfish and manipulative," it feels very personal to Leo. Over time, I've helped him see that the things his mother says aren't actually about Leo. They come from the pain of his mother's childhood.

So how do you get to a place where you don't take things personally? What helps me hold on to this idea is assuming people have good intentions. If someone is doing something that hurts me or someone I love, I decide not to interpret it as their intention.

At first, this might seem like a naïve way to approach the world. Still, I accept the fact that people are going to do or say hurtful things. However, *I choose to see them as unintentional.*

Eventually, I also helped Leo come around to the idea that his mother's behavior was unintentional. Ultimately, his mom wanted to be close to him. So why did she call him selfish and manipulative? Maybe because Leo did something to trigger her, like not calling her very often, which set off her fear that he didn't care. Since it was too painful to face this reality, his mother used anger as a defense. For her, it was easier to see Leo as flawed than face the fear that he might not value her.

After taking a step back from his own anger, Leo finally realized that his mother's behavior was coming from a place of pain. Her anger was a negative coping mechanism. It wasn't about him.

Why is this empowering? It goes back to the idea of having control over your emotions, which we explored at the end of chapter 1. If you're not interpreting other people's behavior as an attack on you, they don't have the ability to hurt you.

If you know what they're saying or doing is not about you, they can't make you angry or make you feel small. That's a powerful place to live.

HOW TO COMMUNICATE WHEN YOU'RE ANGRY

All the ideas we've explored so far in this chapter come into play when you're trying to communicate in moments of anger. Understanding that anger is a secondary emotion, finding your fear, being aware of when you're confusing anger with assertiveness, recognizing when you or others might be intellectualizing anger through judgment, and not taking things personally are all important ideas to hold onto when you're involved in a conflict.

So how do you actually apply these ideas in a situation where you're angry? Let's look at the answer to that question through the lens of our opening story of Joley and her best friend Erin.

STEP BACK AND SLOW DOWN

Joley's first instinct was to swallow her anger after reading Erin's comment on social media. Though I encouraged her to communicate her feelings, I also knew she had to work through her anger before she did that.

Though you don't want to bury your feelings or get stuck in negative emotions, it's not a good idea to communicate when you're angry. If you're in an argument with someone and you're feeling angry, you're in a place of self-protection. You've decided on some level that the other person is the attacker. When you're in this state, there's nothing they can say or do to make you feel better.

As a society, we've evolved to the point where we're expressing our feelings and valuing that expression more than in past generations. While it's important to be honest, if you're yelling, calling someone names, or saying hurtful things you don't really mean, you can do damage that's difficult to repair. Even if you're only feeling them in the moment, painful words can stick in people's minds long after an argument is over.

Before Joley communicated her feelings, I wanted her to shift from seeing Erin as her attacker to seeing her as a human being. How could she do that? The first step was to slow down and step away from the situation.

My number one rule on how to communicate effectively when you're feeling angry is **never communicate when you're feeling a sense of urgency**. The more you feel like you have to say _____, the more important it is to stop and reflect.

When you're in a situation where you feel angry and hurt, the best thing you can do is tell the other person you need a moment. Hang up the phone. Take a walk around the block. Take time to go underneath the anger and think about what's making you feel vulnerable or afraid. Again, simply being aware that you're feeling fear—and acknowledging that fear with acceptance and love—will allow some of it to release.

PICK A GOOD TIME AND PLACE TO COMMUNICATE

After she gave herself time to reflect on the emotions underneath her anger, and no longer saw Erin as her attacker,

Joley needed to find the right time and place to communicate her feelings.

She decided to do it during an upcoming road trip. Months earlier, she and Erin had planned a weekend getaway with their friends. Before they joined the rest of the group, they'd be alone together in the car for a couple of hours. The ride would give Joley plenty of undistracted time and space to express her feelings.

In the meantime, Joley interacted with Erin as usual, texting, chatting, and sending photos back and forth the way she normally did. When they saw each other, Joley felt relatively at ease. After they got in the car together, Joley waited until they'd had a chance to be in each other's presence for a while. By the time she brought up her feelings around Erin's social media comment, they were both in a place of feeling their love and connection for one another.

DON'T GET ATTACHED TO THE OUTCOME

When you're ready to communicate your feelings with someone, it's important to approach it without being attached to the outcome. If you go in feeling like the other person has to respond in a certain way in order for you to feel like things are resolved, you're doomed from the start.

It's also important to be clear that a conflict doesn't have to mean the end of a relationship. By the time she was ready to talk to Erin, Joley had already decided the issue wasn't going to end their friendship.

Joley couldn't control how Erin reacted to what she was

going to say. What she could do was choose to be empathetic and try to see things from her friend's perspective. She also reminded herself of all the ways Erin had shown her love in the past.

Joley didn't start off the conversation by saying, "I'm still with you. This doesn't change our relationship. It doesn't matter what you say. We're best friends." But Erin could feel that intention behind her words, which helped clear a path for the two of them to communicate in a deep, loving, honest way.

KEEP IT SIMPLE

We're not used to communicating with each other on a deep level, so the quicker we can get to the point, the less time it gives the other person's negative mind voice to come up with a scary story about what's happening. Using short sentences is helpful, too.

Here's how Joley kept it simple: "You know what? I saw your post on Instagram the other day. To be honest, when I saw it made me kind of scared that you don't understand my experience or that of other people of color. I'm not bringing this up to make you feel bad or to shame you. I just feel like this is the first time in my life I'm able to talk about my experiences as a Filipino woman. When you said you think people are being overly sensitive, it made me feel like you don't see me. And I don't want us to stop sharing what our experience is."

"Oh, my God," Erin said. "That wasn't my intention at all. I would never want to silence your voice. Here's what was happening for me that day..."

From there, the two of them were able to have a deep, sincere conversation. Erin told Joley about her struggles being the only white person at her job. The Instagram post came from her feelings of being isolated. She asked Joley how to connect better with her colleagues at work. They brainstormed ways to improve the situation.

After their conversation, Erin felt even closer to Joley. On top of that, Joley eventually helped Erin turn things around at her job. Had Joley not brought up how that social media post had affected her, none of this would have happened.

Joley's experience shows how you can transform yourself as well as your relationships when you learn to express the true feelings beneath your anger.

However, if you're suffering from depression, it can be a struggle to figure out what your true feelings actually are. In chapter 3, we'll look at ways to ease depression.

PRACTICE

Think about a time when you felt angry recently. Take ten minutes to write about it. Don't censor yourself.

Reread what you've written. See if you can identify the fear underneath your anger.

Can you identify other times in your life when this fear came up? Can you trace your fear back to an experience you had in childhood?

Is your root fear connected to a survival-related fear, like getting kicked out of your tribe or not being able to meet your basic needs?

Now take some time to journal about what you need in order to soothe the fear. Can you give it to yourself? For example, can you hold on to the idea that the people you care about have good intentions for you? Can you replay your recent interactions and notice the ways your loved ones demonstrated their positive feelings for you? Is there a different way to look at the situation around the person you're angry with that takes you out of self-protective mode—and gives you a deeper understanding of their perspective?

If you don't feel better after taking yourself through these steps, you may need input from someone else. In that case, return to the final section in this chapter about how to communicate when you feel angry.

CHAPTER 3

HOW TO EASE DEPRESSION

By the time he came to me for therapy, Rob had attempted suicide multiple times. He was in his early twenties, living with his dog in an apartment his mother was paying for. He wasn't working or going to school. Since he couldn't bring himself to take a shower, he smelled like sweat and body odor. He felt isolated from his family and from everyone else in his life.

"I feel like a loser," he said. "In my family, I'm a waste of space."

He constantly compared himself to his brother, who had a great career, a girlfriend, and a good body. His mother, a brilliant lawyer, yelled at him constantly, telling him to do something with his life. His father was out of the picture. After Rob stole Vicodin and other prescription medication from his mom and step-father, they got angry with him for breaking their trust.

In the beginning, he came to my office four days a week. Of all the cases I've worked, his felt like the most dangerous. He was teetering between life and death. I worried about him overdosing on Vicodin; I was afraid I might lose him. There were many days when he couldn't bring himself to leave his apartment. So we talked on the phone.

His own emotions terrified him. He rejected the idea of letting himself feel the depth of his sadness; he thought it would destroy him. The more he resisted it, though, the more intense it became.

Rob was drowning in depression.

WHAT IS DEPRESSION?

We often think of depression as feeling sad or down. However, depression actually comes from holding on to our negative emotions—and then judging ourselves for feeling them.

When we feel depressed, it's because we've swallowed our feelings. They're stuck inside us.

So it's actually the act of denying our emotions that causes us to feel sad, or angry, or apathetic. When we tell ourselves, like Rob did, that it's not okay to feel sad or upset, depression grows.

In other words, feelings of intense sadness, fear, or vulnerability are not the depression itself. These feelings come along, but then we judge them, deny them, or don't let ourselves experience them. Depression is the end result of repeating this emotional process hundreds or thousands of times.

IS DEPRESSION A DISEASE?

In chapter 1, I mentioned the idea of taking ownership of anxiety by thinking of it as something unique to us. We talk about "my anxiety" as if it's part of our identity. We tend to do the same thing with depression.

Instead of looking at it as a symptom of something that's not functioning correctly in our emotional system, we think of "my depression" as a disease.

I disagree with this idea. Classifying depression as a disease implies that it's something we can't fix. Whereas if we say to ourselves, "I have this depression. It's valid. It's real. It's intense. It's hard. I don't know how to get out of it, but I also know it isn't me," we're telling ourselves it's possible to change our relationship with it.

IS DEPRESSION GENETIC?

If everyone in your family has depression, you could be predisposed to depression. However, and I know this is controversial, I think depression has more to with the environment we grow up in than with genetics. When the people around us are depressed, it's how we learn to cope— or not to cope—with our feelings.

It's a scientific fact that certain things get passed down genetically or physically from generation to generation. However, we don't often consider the idea that emotional processes get passed down, too. The ways our family members expressed emotion, not to mention the ways they communicated, have a powerful influence on us.

For example, my parents were raised by parents who didn't know how to deal with their negative feelings. If times were tough, they had no choice but to "keep calm and carry on." In other words, they grew up learning to repress their feelings of sadness. By the time I was born, my parents had evolved somewhat, but they still passed on the idea that it wasn't okay to be upset. They didn't do it intentionally. I knew they loved me, but I grew up internalizing the idea that my feelings weren't acceptable. After my cousins died, those feelings got stuck, and there was nowhere for them to go. That's depression.

The Oscar-winning documentary *Three Identical Strangers* is another example of how profoundly our families' emotional processes can impact us. It follows the individual lives of male triplets who are separated six months after birth and grow up in three different families. Though their genetics are identical, each one learns to cope with his emotions in different ways.

As they transition from childhood to adulthood, all three of them struggle with their mental health. However, only one of the triplets, Eddy, ends up committing suicide. Of the three families, his parents turn out to be the least emotionally accepting. Though it's obvious they love him, it's clear that they don't know how to express and feel their emotions. This leaves Eddy feeling alone. Since he doesn't develop the emotional tools to cope with his sadness or his fear, he decides to take his own life.

OTHER SOURCES OF DEPRESSION

The experience you have with your immediate family isn't the only reason you might be predisposed to depression. Your community and your culture can also play a part. Maybe you live in a war-torn country. Perhaps you grew up surrounded by alcoholics or drug addicts. You might come from a culture where expressing emotion is taboo. Your problems don't develop in a vacuum. If everyone around you feels pain, it exacerbates your own.

You can also trace depression back to your negative mind. Again, once you meet your basic survival needs, this is the negative voice that fills the empty space in your mind with thoughts and emotions designed to keep you alive. When you're feeling anxious, the negative mind puts you in a hyper-vigilant state. When you're feeling depressed, though, the negative mind encourages you to isolate yourself. It's basically saying that the best way to survive is to crawl in a hole and not come out until you're ready to deal with the world.

In other words, if you're feeling depressed, and all you want to do is be alone, there's nothing wrong with you. You're just following your survival instinct, which is behaving as if you still live in the jungle, where you need to hide out and heal your wounds to escape potential predators.

However, in depression, and in many other situations in life, your survival instinct isn't always your best guide. So where can you turn if you can't trust your instincts? We'll explore this idea later on in this chapter.

HOW DO YOU KNOW IF YOU'RE DEPRESSED?

Everyone experiences depression differently, and the symptoms vary from person to person. That said, the following are the symptoms of depression, according to the Diagnostic and Statistical Manual of Mental Disorders (DSM-V) published by the American Psychiatric Association. According to the DSM-V, you may be suffering from depression if you experience five or more of these symptoms during the same two-week period (and if one of these symptoms is either depressed mood or loss of interest or pleasure):

- Depressed mood most of the day, nearly every day.
- Diminished interest or loss of pleasure in all, or almost all, activities most of the day, nearly every day.
- Significant weight loss when not dieting, or weight gain, or decrease or increase in appetite nearly every day.
- A slowing down of thought and a reduction of physical movement (observable by others, not merely subjective feelings of restlessness or being slowed down).
- Fatigue or loss of energy nearly every day.
- Feelings of worthlessness or excessive or inappropriate guilt nearly every day.
- Diminished ability to think or concentrate, or indecisiveness, nearly every day.
- Recurrent thoughts of death, recurrent suicidal ideation without a specific plan, or a suicide attempt or a specific plan for committing suicide.

If one or more of these symptoms applies to you, think of them as a description of how you're feeling—not as a disease or a problem that can't be fixed.

HOW TO ALLEVIATE DEPRESSION

Alleviating depression starts with accepting the feelings you're having. The more you can surrender and express, instead of *de*press, the more your emotions will organically move through you. This is what emotions are supposed to do.

Your emotions are temporary. They're designed to flow through you like a river. If you feel depressed, though, you've basically built a dam that stops the flow of your feelings. Over time, the pressure builds. If you break the dam, you're afraid you'll drown in your feelings—or lose the ability to function. That's the story your negative mind is telling you, but it's not true.

So how do you develop the ability to experience your emotions?

REPARENTING

The idea of expressing stuck feelings is a very modern concept. This is what I tell most of my young adult clients, including Rob, whose story opens this chapter. Because it's such a new idea, there's a good chance that the adults in your life somehow communicated the message that you're better off swallowing your feelings.

However, if this is the emotional process you learned in childhood, you can also learn to let go of it. As an adult, it's possible to teach yourself a new way to deal with your feelings. In other words, you can reparent yourself.

What does reparenting involve? It starts with teaching yourself to accept whatever you're feeling. It's about learning to give yourself permission to experience emotions like sadness, frustration, doubt, and fear *as you experience them*, instead of judging yourself for having them.

As I was struggling with depression, reparenting was how I started to release it. When a feeling of sadness came over me, I tried to sit in the emotion, giving myself an immense amount of empathy and compassion. I treated myself the way I'd treat someone I loved. I hugged myself. I stroked my arms. I used soothing words: "It's okay to be sad," I told myself. "It's okay to be scared."

With his father out of the picture and his mother physically but not emotionally present, Rob eventually learned to reparent himself, too. At first, it was hard for him to allow himself to feel. He was convinced he wasn't strong enough to feel his emotions. Gradually, as he learned to lean into his feelings, we also took baby steps to improve his daily life to support the reparenting process.

CHANGE THE ENVIRONMENT

Whenever I work with clients who are feeling depressed, our initial goal is to get out of the house every day. This was how I approached the sessions with Rob. At first, his only activity was to come to my office to talk with me.

Why is it important to change your environment? As I mentioned above, when you're feeling depressed, your instinct is to isolate yourself. Interacting with people and being in the world seems to take an enormous amount of energy. But it's the best thing you can do when you're feeling depressed. By changing your environment and breaking up your routine, you start to move the energy in your body. This also moves the energy in your mind.

Depression is the emotional equivalent of being stuck in the mud. When you get out of bed, leave the house, spend time in nature, or visit someone, you're letting the negative energy in your body move through you instead of letting it build up inside.

If you've been feeling depressed for a long time, I understand how difficult it is to get yourself to move. It's the last thing you want to do. The key is to figure out the easiest thing you're capable of doing right now. Can you take a five-minute walk? Can you do a ten-minute yoga video? It doesn't even have to be a "healthy" activity. If buying a soda at 7/11 is the only thing that motivates you to leave the house, try that. The important thing is to move the energy so you can begin to release it. Again, it all starts with baby steps.

SELF-CARE

After it became easier for Rob to leave his apartment, we looked at ways he could take better care of himself physically. He started with taking a shower once a week. Then he progressed to showering once every few days. After that, we worked on having him drink enough water. Eventually, we explored how he could eat better. He started off having a salad a day.

Why is self-care important when you're feeling depressed? It's also part of the process of reparenting yourself, which is an external as much as an internal process. When you do things to take care of yourself physically, like eating healthy food or exercising, you're not just improving your appearance. You're learning to nurture yourself. You're telling yourself you deserve to be well cared for. You're also moving the stagnant energy in your body.

We'll explore more ways to establish a healthy self-care routine in chapter 5.

LET SOMEONE IN

Besides changing your environment and taking care of your physical self, another aspect of alleviating depression involves talking with someone. If you don't have access to a therapist, try to find someone who encourages you and offers unconditional support. Is it a friend? A teacher? A family member? Whoever it is, they should help reinforce the idea that it's okay to feel whatever you're feeling.

Since we tend to isolate ourselves when we're depressed, the experience of sitting with another person and interacting with them is important. Even if you're an introvert, you need to connect with other human beings. When you talk with someone who understands and accepts you, your negative mind automatically quiets down. Even if it's only temporary, having someone hold your hand and believe in you helps ease feelings of depression.

If you don't have someone to help you through your reparenting process, there are other resources you can turn to. For example, many of my clients who are socially isolated find ways to connect with others online. This can mean playing video games that involve collaborating with others, joining an online chat group with people who share a common interest—or joining a group that meets offline if you feel ready to go out into the world.

When you're looking for support, it's sometimes more effective to communicate with people who share your passions instead of your problems. While it's good to find people to whom you can express your true feelings, you don't want negative emotions to be the only basis of your connection with other people.

Though you might connect easily with others who are suffering from depression, those connections sometimes take you to a dark place, making it difficult to move forward. On the other hand, when you start making connections based on your interests, you build relationships on a positive foundation; as you grow closer to people, you can always open up and share more, if and when it feels right.

REPARENT YOURSELF WITH LOVE

Whether it's being with your emotions, changing your environment, moving your body, or making time to talk with someone, the reparenting process only works if you combine your actions with feelings of self-love and acceptance.

Self-love can be challenging at first. It certainly was for Rob. "This is ridiculous!" he would say. "All I did was take a shower. Why should I love myself for that?"

That was his negative mind talking. It's the voice Rob had learned to pay attention to. It's the voice we all learn to pay attention to. This is where we often get stuck.

Over time, I taught Rob to quiet his negative mind by recognizing it for what it was. Little by little, he learned to allow himself to experience his feelings as they came up without judging himself for having them. He also developed the ability to celebrate each baby step he took, especially for practical things like taking a shower or cooking a healthy meal.

IN DEPRESSION, QUESTION YOUR INSTINCTS

When you start taking steps to ease depression, your negative mind will automatically resist, saying things like: "What are you doing? Don't move! Why are you going out? It's dangerous out there."

When we first started working together, if Rob woke up and felt terrible, he could easily persuade himself to stay in bed and watch TV all day.

Initially, he didn't realize that his instincts were leading him in the wrong direction. Like most of us, he'd been taught to trust his instincts. "Well, Jesse," he said. "You told me to pay attention to my inner voice and my true self. And it's saying I need to lie in bed and not see anyone and not move."

But that wasn't his true self talking. It was his negative mind. When you're feeling depressed, your negative mind, disguised as your instincts, often tells you the opposite of what you actually need. It goes into overdrive to protect and conserve all your energy—because you think you don't have any.

However, unless you have a medical condition, your body probably does have physical energy. What you lack is psychological energy.

So how do you know when your instincts are leading you

astray? How can you distinguish between your negative mind and your true self? Think about what you would tell a friend. Imagine your friend was lying in bed all day, eating junk food, not talking to anyone, and having a tough time in general. Would you say, "It's okay. Just keep doing what you're doing. You'll feel better eventually"?

I don't think so.

Your true self is always going to guide you toward things that move you forward. It's never going to give you negative feedback or encourage you to do things that keep you down.

DO, THEN DISTRACT

I understand that there's a difference between knowing intellectually that it's a good idea to take a walk, eat a salad, or talk to a friend and finding the internal strength to do these things.

One way to motivate yourself to take a baby step is to give yourself permission to return to your resting state afterward. After you take yourself to the park or pick up ingredients for a healthy meal at the store, go back to lying in bed, binge-watching your favorite TV show, or doing whatever you usually do to distract or soothe yourself.

You're not trying to go from not showering or leaving the house one day to eating three healthy meals, taking a bath, and meeting a friend the next. The goal is to choose one thing you can do today to help release the depression, be positive about taking that step, and then go back to lying in bed.

Then, while you're lying in bed, continue the process of reparenting yourself. Instead of telling yourself you're stuck and can't move, embrace what you're doing. For example: "I'm going to enjoy this Netflix show right now. And tomorrow I'm going to walk ten minutes instead of five."

In other words, if you're doing something to distract or soothe yourself, try to enjoy it and be in it fully. When you approach your distractions in a positive, mindful way as you inch toward your goals, you'll find that you need them less and less.

FEEL, THEN DISTRACT

If you reach a point in the reparenting process when your feelings are overwhelming, there are things you can do to manage the pain. As I was struggling with depression, journaling helped me in moments when my emotions felt unbearable. Writing things down allowed me to release my feelings as they came to me. For a little while, I gave myself permission to feel whatever the emotion was. Then I took myself to the movies. Sitting in the theater helped me escape my negative emotional state for a few hours.

It's the same principle I was discussing above. Besides *doing* then distracting, you can also *feel* then distract. In both cases, you're giving yourself a break from your mind. You're also empowering yourself to control how fast your feelings come out. Like a good parent, you're setting the terms.

ANTI-DEPRESSANTS

Though people are quick to prescribe them in this country, I look at anti-depressants as a last resort. If you're feeling suicidal, if you're suffering to the point where you're physically and emotionally paralyzed, or if you're trying to reparent yourself and taking baby steps to ease depression but you still can't move, anti-depressants are certainly an option.

On the other hand, if you're thinking about turning to anti-depressants instead of working to change your relationship with your emotions, my experience is that they usually don't work. And I've tried them all.

Anti-depressants are designed to encourage the flow of serotonin, the feel-good hormone, into your brain synapses. Though you may feel the benefits of that serotonin in your mind and body at first, those benefits generally don't last if you're not learning to accept and feel your feelings. Why not?

Anti-depressants don't get rid of the negative voice in your head. They may turn down the volume a little, but if you haven't done the work to understand that it's in your power to shift your emotional state, they're practically useless.

CHOOSE YOUR LIFE

As a teenager, I started to think of suicide as an exit strategy after I lost my cousins. Even after I started therapy, I always held suicide as a possibility in the back of my mind. "If things get really bad," I thought, "I'll just kill myself."

I had a ready supply of sleeping pills. Just knowing they were there made me feel less trapped.

When I turned eighteen, besides seeing Toni, the therapist

who changed my life, I also went to group therapy. One day we did an exercise where we wrote down something we thought each member of the group needed to know to improve their life. When it came to me, everyone wrote down the same thing: "You're a victim of your life."

Those words hit me hard. I'd survived so many painful experiences by then. I considered myself strong, not a victim.

I went home that night and planned to take the pills. "They don't understand everything I've been through," I thought. "Now they'll see how they hurt me."

As I held the jar of pills in my hand, a thought came into my head: the people in the group were on my side. Maybe they were trying to tell me something valuable? I sank to the bathroom floor, closing my eyes. I tried to breathe deeply.

In the middle of a long exhale, I had an epiphany: I didn't need death as an option to be free. I was already free. I didn't have to do anything I didn't want to do.

I stood up and flushed the sleeping pills down the toilet.

Until then, I hadn't understood that keeping one foot out the door would get me nowhere. As long as suicide was an option, I would never figure out how to be fully present in my life. If I couldn't choose to be here, how could I create the life I wanted?

Choosing to live your life is the starting point for all of the depression-easing strategies I've talked about in this chapter. If you can't commit to your life right now, then it's important to seek therapy and potentially take anti-depressants until you arrive at the point where you know you want to be here.

ROB'S TRANSFORMATION

I knew Rob was ready to commit to his life when he handed over his supply of Vicodin. By then, he'd started taking baby steps to ease the depression: showering regularly, eating healthier, and reconnecting with his old friends one at a time. But things truly started to change for him when he surrendered those pain pills.

Our conversations shifted. We went from focusing on how awful his life was to celebrating his victories, no matter how small they seemed. Eventually, he brought up his love of soccer. Before he'd gotten severely depressed, he'd played on a professional soccer team. He wondered whether he might be able to transform his passion for the sport into something larger.

We took baby steps here, too. We started off with him taking a soccer ball out of his closet. Then we built up to having him kick the ball against the garage door. He graduated to taking the ball to the park and practicing on his own. After a few months of going to the park, he worked up the courage to join a pick-up game.

Before long, he decided to coach a community soccer team for kids ten and under. The parents were so impressed with his coaching skills that they started asking him for private coaching sessions. His team won the league championship. Pretty soon, parents from other teams started to seek him out for private coaching. One connection led to another. His sport was giving him a sense of purpose and fulfillment.

As time went on, Rob came to see me less and less. In soccer, he discovered something he could hold onto that wasn't dark. Today he's a successful coach who manages a competitive club soccer program; many of his former players have gone on to win athletic scholarships and play professionally.

Rob has become the best version of himself. His negative thought patterns are still there, but he's developed the skills to cope with them. Instead of believing everything his negative mind is telling him, he's learned to listen to the voice of his true self.

Learning to separate the voice of your negative mind from that of your true self takes practice. Meditation is the easiest way to do this, and we'll explore how in the next chapter, along with examining other methods to find calm and focus on the big picture of your life.

PRACTICE

Make a list of five baby steps you can take to change your emotional state right now.

Take a week and choose one thing on this list that you're going to do every day to make yourself feel a bit better. It can be anything from taking a walk around the block, taking a shower, meditating for one minute, eating a healthy meal, doing five minutes of yoga, or talking to a friend.

The important things are 1) to pick something feels challenging but is still doable for you right now, and 2) to write it on your calendar (writing things down increases the likelihood that you'll do them).

Every time you take a baby step to make yourself feel better, note it on your calendar. Then acknowledge yourself. Besides addressing yourself in an encouraging way (e.g., "Even though it was hard, you moved today, and that's amazing!"), be sure to reward yourself every time you do what you've committed to, whether that means going back to bed, playing video games, or watching your favorite TV show.

After the week is over, take a few minutes to note how you feel. Do you notice any difference in your emotional state? If so, keep going with this baby step. If not, choose a different one.

Gradually, as you continue to take baby steps and reward yourself, your list will become longer and your steps bigger. For now, the key is to pick the easiest thing you can do right now to make yourself feel better. Then do it, recognize yourself for doing it—and repeat it. Along the way, make a note every time you catch yourself standing up against a negative thought and saying something loving to yourself instead.

CHAPTER 4

HOW TO TAKE CARE
OF YOUR SPIRIT

When I introduced you to my client Diego in chapter 1, he was suffering from severe anxiety. At nineteen years old, after dropping out of school, breaking up with his girlfriend, and distancing himself from his friends, he'd reached a low point in his life. To ease his social insecurity and disconnect from his pain, he smoked pot.

After a particularly bad trip at a party one night, Diego decided to give up marijuana. By the time he came to see me, he was sober, though he was at a loss when it came to dealing with his feelings. But he was attracted to the idea of meditation.

Though he thought it would be good for his mind, he struggled to start a meditation practice. He could only stand to sit still for one minute at a time. Eventually, as I wrote in chapter 1, he dragged himself to a meditation meet-up. Over time, he learned to do longer and longer sits.

Meditation was becoming a source of relief for him. He felt moments of peace. After months of isolation, he was becoming part of a community. Then things changed.

As he went deeper and deeper into his practice, his negative emotions started to release. The fears and traumas he'd been stuffing away for so long started to overtake his meditations. He went from "everything's looking better!" to feeling suicidal.

"I don't know if I can go on," he told me. He didn't understand what was happening to him. He wanted to give up his meditation practice. That's just what his negative mind wanted him to do.

OUR NEGATIVE MINDS

As I wrote in chapter 1, our minds aren't designed to keep us happy or at peace. They're designed to keep us alive. Again, this goes back to the fact that we've out-evolved our negative mind. Though we no longer live in the wild or have to fight for our survival on a daily basis, our minds don't know that. They're still trying to keep us alive. And the best way to do that is to keep us in a fearful, hyper-vigilant state.

Your negative mind is rooted in your survival instinct, but it's also fueled by your experience. It focuses on *your* specific triggers in order to keep you in a state of anxiousness. If you survived something painful or learned unhealthy emotional processes in childhood, certain situations in adulthood will trigger your pain.

As Diego went deeper into his meditation practice, he came

face to face with his own triggers, which were rooted in his experience of being a child of divorced parents. "I'm a loser," he told himself. "I don't know how to connect with people. I'm going to be alone for the rest of my life." When those thoughts came into his head, sadness and fear followed.

What Diego struggled to understand was that we all have triggers that unleash negative thoughts and emotions. Sooner or later, all of us face people or situations that push our buttons.

Though it was hard for him to grasp the idea initially, Diego eventually understood that there was nothing wrong with feeling sadness or fear—and that there was nothing wrong with him. Ultimately, the negative voice in his head, like the negative voice in all our heads, was part of being human.

HOW TO TURN DOWN THE VOLUME ON THE NEGATIVE MIND

The first step in turning down the volume on the negative mind is admitting it's there.

The second step is to understand that most of the time your mind isn't telling you the truth about what's happening right now. Again, its job is to look for the thought that's going to activate your negative emotions and focus in on that thought.

Growing up, you learn to accept your thoughts as facts. When you're feeling anxious, you can often trace the anxiety back to a survival-related fear like getting kicked out of your tribe. In the past, getting kicked out of your tribe meant being in danger of not having the resources to feed yourself, as well as not having the means to shelter yourself from the elements and/or predatory animals. This is why it can feel like life or death on an emotional level when you're in a situation where you feel rejected, or when other people hurt your feelings—even though you know intellectually that the stakes aren't that high.

When you're depressed, your negative mind tells you it's better to sit still, because this keeps you out of physical or emotional danger. When you feel hurt, you think the pain will last forever. But these are just stories your mind is telling you. They're not true. More often than not, they're based on a survival-related fear that doesn't correspond with your current reality.

When you understand where the stories in your mind are coming from, you can start to give less weight to the negative thoughts in your head.

In other words, don't believe everything you think.

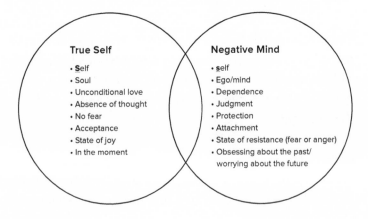

SEPARATING THE NEGATIVE MIND AND YOUR TRUE SELF

How do you know when your mind isn't telling you the truth? And how can you keep your mind from misleading you? The key is to teach yourself to recognize when the negative mind is doing the talking.

As we discussed in chapter 1, we all have two selves: our true self and our negative mind. Again, as the graphic shows, your true self manifests in feelings like joy, presence, connection, and peace. Meanwhile, the negative mind takes the form of feelings like fear, judgment, and dependence.

Once you start to recognize the difference between your true self and your negative mind, you can practice being aware in the moments when your negative mind takes over.

How do you know when your negative mind is taking over? It's actually a two-part process. First, your mind comes up with a negative thought. Secondly, you have an emotional reaction to that thought, which could be fear, anger, or judgment.

When you notice yourself getting stuck in a negative thought loop, kindly tell your mind, "Thank you for trying to protect me, but I'm okay. And I don't need to be assessing danger right now."

When you learn to recognize the voice of your negative mind and the emotions it brings up, they start to lose their power over you. Instead of holding on to painful thoughts and emotions, you grow less attached to them. You begin to see your situation for what it is.

IDENTIFY YOUR TRIGGERS

All of us have triggers that set our negative minds in motion, keeping us in an anxious and/or aroused state. Triggers are the way your negative mind talks to you. Once you identify them, it becomes easier to see when your negative mind is taking over.

Everyone's triggers are different. For my clients, needing approval from others, not meeting their or others' expectations for success, or jealousy can be common triggers. "I'm not good enough, I'm not smart enough, I'm all alone, I'm never going to have enough money to have the kind of life I want[3]": these are the kinds of thoughts that come from our triggers.

How do you identify your triggers? By paying attention. By looking for patterns. What are the negative thoughts, and/or the emotionally-charged situations, that keep coming up for you?

Do you ever feel like little things make you extremely upset? If someone doesn't respond to one of your texts, for example, do you tend to overreact? Even though your intellect is telling you it's no big deal that X isn't answering you, it can feel like a life-or-death scenario. Why? Because your mind is zeroing in on your survival-related fear of getting kicked out of your tribe. However, once you learn to recognize this triggering thought, you can stop it from taking over your emotions.

---

3   Even though most of us know intellectually that we're probably not in danger being homeless or starving to death, not having enough money can sometimes feel like a life-or-death scenario. In this case, our emotional reactions are rooted in our survival-related fear of not having enough resources.

MEDITATION IS THE EASIEST WAY—BUT NOT THE ONLY WAY

Meditation is the easiest way to train yourself to recognize when your triggers are activating your negative mind. It's also the simplest way to see and feel the separation between the negative mind and your true self. If you're ready to learn about starting a meditation practice, turn to Chapter 4. If you want to learn about other techniques for calming the negative mind, continue reading.

Ultimately, meditation isn't the only way to quiet the negative mind.

In fact, the first time I tried to meditate, I felt like I was going to crawl out of my skin. Meditating for one minute was torture for me. Feeling depressed and anxious made it impossible to sit still. So I searched for alternatives to meditation that helped me find calm, stay focused on the big picture, and connect with my true self.

TRUE-SELF ACTIVITIES

Before I developed a meditation practice, the easiest way to connect with my true self was to make time to do the things I loved. When I went snowboarding, for example, and I was standing outside on the mountain, I was immediately in my true self. I felt happy, strong, and glad to be alive.

Cooking gave me a similar feeling. When I was chopping herbs or tasting as I went along, I didn't worry about the future or obsess about the past. I was literally savoring the moment, engaging my senses, and paying close attention to everything I was doing.

Our true-self activities don't have to be as involved as snowboarding or cooking. They can be as simple as taking a walk in the park, spending time with a friend, or going to the movies.

If you're looking for calm and happiness, it's important to find things that inspire and relax you, and bring you into the moment. These are the things that help you connect with your true self.

Once you find your true-self activities, try to make time for them on a daily basis. Why? The more time you spend in your true self, the easier it is for you to access those positive emotions when you need them. Think of it as creating emotional muscle memory. The more you work the true-self muscle, the stronger it becomes over time.

When you're doing something challenging, like networking or having an honest conversation with your parents/caregivers, you go back to the thoughts and emotions your mind is used to. The more you can draw on the emotional muscle memory of your true self, the easier it is to bring the best version of yourself to those situations.

BRAIN-CALMING GAMES

Besides meditation, there are plenty of other things you can do to activate the same parts of your brain that meditation does—including games.

In her book *SuperBetter*, game designer Jane McGonigal shares the story of how she used games to recover from a severe concussion that made her feel suicidal. Though she was physically incapacitated, she decided to create a make-believe game called "Jane the Concussion-Slayer" to keep herself motivated during her recovery process.

The deeper she got into designing the game, the more McGonigal realized she was building resilience and optimism that translated into her real life. She also found that playing games (including but not limited to video games) put her in a state of flow that took her out of her negative mind.

When she shared her findings with the wider world, McGonigal discovered that other people also experienced the meditation-like effects of playing games. On top of that, she found that certain games, like Tetris and Candy Crush Saga, could even help prevent or reduce symptoms of post-traumatic stress disorder (PTSD).[4]

Besides playing games, McGonigal came up with a series of other simple, doable meditation-simulating activities. Each is designed to help you focus on the task at hand and calm your mind.[5]

4   Jane McGonigal. "Play, don't replay! HELP PREVENT PTSD." Janemcgonigal.com/2014/03/27/
    help-prevent-ptsd (retrieved December 17, 2019)

5   Jane McGonigal, *SuperBetter: The Power of Living Gamefully* (New York: Penguin, 2015).

MIND-CALMING ACTIVITIES

One-Minute Breathing: Breathe in for a count of four and breathe out for a count of eight for at least one minute. Breathing this way increases your heart rate variability (the difference in the length of time between your heartbeats), which soothes your nervous system in the short term and protects against stress, anxiety, pain, and inflammation over the long term.

The Pink Elephant: Spend one minute trying **not** to think about a pink elephant. Note how often you thought about the pink elephant during that minute. Now try again for one minute, but this time, list as many words as you can starting with "P" and "E." Note how much listing the words helped take your mind off the pink elephant. When you're trying to ease depression or anxiety, or fight cravings, this technique helps train your mind to focus on one source of information at a time and ignore everything else, which can improve how you feel.

YOGA

I was able to do yoga long before I was able to meditate. If you're not ready to sit with your thoughts, yoga is a great place to start because it helps shift your focus away from your negative thought patterns and onto your body and breath. It also moves stagnant energy in the body, which is one of the keys to releasing depression and other negative emotions.

Which type of yoga should you choose? The one you're most attracted to. Even if you lean toward fitness-focused yoga versus more spiritually oriented yoga, you'll still learn to focus on your breath and stay in the present moment. Both of these skills are important in terms of helping to calm the negative mind and strengthen the connection with your true self.

SO WHY MEDITATE?

As I wrote in the introduction, the most powerful approach to self-transformation merges aspects of psychology and spirituality. Psychology did help me cope with anxiety and depression. In the end, though, it was meditation that led me to a new level of joy and fulfillment. How?

Even though my analytical mind was attracted to the process of dissecting my feelings from a psychological perspective, it was impossible to dissect all the negative thoughts I had every day. Meditation gave me the tools to feel then release negative emotions. It helped me realize I didn't have to spend so much time in my head digging for the roots of my thoughts.

Still, when I started meditating, I could only do it for one minute every day. During that minute, I set the intention to listen to the difference between my negative mind and my true self. Noticing the difference automatically turned the volume down on my negative mind. Over time, as I extended my meditation sessions, I started giving less and less value to the negative voice in my head.

I also discovered that if I breathed and sat with my feelings, observing them instead of resisting them, I could actually witness them moving through me. The more I meditated, the easier it was to understand the idea that our emotions are impermanent—and to bring that understanding into my daily life.

At the same time, meditation also made it easier to recognize where I was getting emotionally stuck, and see where I wanted to dig more deeply from a psychological perspective, outside of my meditation sessions. This is when I first learned about the power of merging aspects of psychology and spirituality.

During meditation, I noticed that the same triggers came up for me over and over again: I didn't have value, and I didn't deserve love. Throughout my meditation sessions, I let myself feel those feelings. After my sessions, I decided to look more closely at these triggers from a psychological standpoint.

How? I wrote in my journal. I mined my childhood, and my experiences in adulthood. I shared my experiences with people I trusted. Once I figured out that the emotional patterns I learned in childhood were the source of my triggers, I could start to release them. We'll explore this idea in more depth in chapter 10.

In the meantime, we need to work both the psychological and spiritual sides if we want to transform ourselves. Again, imagine a scenario where you've been rolling around in the mud (the mud representing your pain). If you want to clean yourself off, you need to do it in two stages. The first is hosing off the surface dirt, which is the equivalent of what meditation can do for us. The second stage is scrubbing at the stubborn spots in the shower, which is the function of psychology.

Ultimately, meditation fractioned the amount of time I had to spend to get to the core of a problem. Thanks to what's become a daily meditation practice, I've developed the ability to acknowledge my emotions and let them flow through me. At the same time, I've learned to recognize when I need to continue the emotional work outside of my meditation sessions. The more I meditate, the easier it is to see the world as I want to experience it—and spend more time in my true self.

MISCONCEPTIONS ABOUT MEDITATION

If you're thinking about starting a meditation practice, it's helpful to understand what it is—and what it isn't. Even though meditation is becoming more and more popular in the Western world, we still have quite a few misconceptions about it. Let's clear up a few popular myths about meditation.

Myth #1: You have to do it for a long time. If you were a couch potato and you decided to train for a marathon, you wouldn't start by running twenty miles. You'd start by walking a quarter of a mile. The same is true for meditation. You can start with three deep breaths a day. You can start doing it for one minute a day, like I did. The key is to be honest with yourself about what your edge is. Figure out what's challenging but doable for you. If it's three deep breaths a day, that's still beneficial.

Myth #2: The voice in your head is too loud. If you feel like your negative mind is talking to you all the time, meditation can be especially helpful for you. As challenging as it is, you want to listen to what your mind is telling you so you can begin to separate the negative mind from your true self.

Myth #3: You're bad at meditation. This goes along with Myth #2. *No one* is good at meditation. It's a challenge for all of us. However, most of the time the people who think they're the worst at it are the ones who could benefit the most from it. The harder it is for you, the more crucial it is to do it. I'm a prime example. The fact that meditation was torture for me was proof of how loud my negative mind voice was. It was also evidence of how ingrained I was in that perspective.

Myth #4: The goal of meditation is not to think. The goal of meditation isn't to completely quiet your mind. Though you can have moments of not thinking, the goal is actually to get to a place where you can recognize the difference between your negative mind and your true self. Again, if all you do is sit for one minute each day and observe how your mind talks to you, you'll still see the benefits.

Myth #5: Meditation is an "out-there," esoteric concept. Some of my clients associate the word "meditation" with the new age movement. In reality, people who meditate are just working to separate their negative mind from their true self. Though many of the world's religions incorporate meditation into their practices, meditation is something you can do no matter what you believe (or don't believe).

HOW TO START A MEDITATION PRACTICE

Now that you have a better idea about what meditation involves, let's look at how to start and stay committed to a meditation practice.

- Find a quiet, comfortable place where you won't be disturbed.

- Sit on a cushion on the floor with your legs crossed, or

in a chair with your back straight yet relaxed. If you're feeling anxious, lie down on your back (but try not to fall asleep!).

🖋 Take a few deep breaths. Sit still for a minute, observing your inhales and exhales. Try inhaling to a count of four and exhaling to a count of eight.

🖋 **Practice seeing what your mind is saying to you.** When you meditate, try to see the words that pop into your mind without immediately assigning meaning to them. Instead of attaching yourself to a thought or a feeling, try observing it from the outside.

Treat your thoughts like data in a science experiment. For example, let's imagine the words, "Nobody likes me," come into your mind. You can let those words go. You don't have to analyze or reconcile them right now. Those words are a trigger. They're coming from your negative mind, which is pulling that trigger to bring you back into survival mode.

Ultimately, the goal is to observe your thoughts without judging or attaching to them—and note your emotional reaction to them. However, sometimes you may not be able to hear the thoughts, even though you feel the negative feelings they're bringing up. If you continue to meditate, you'll learn to let those feelings move through you without judging yourself for having them.

🖋 **Practice the noting technique.** When you first start meditating, you might find it difficult to focus. In this case, the noting technique can help you sustain your attention. Whenever you see, hear, think, or feel something that distracts you from your breath, consciously name it. For example, if your mind wanders to some construction noise outside, you can mentally say, "hearing, hearing, hearing" until you can bring yourself back to the present moment. If you sense pain in your body, mentally say "feeling" until your awareness stabilizes. At first, your practice might sound something like "see, see, feel, feel, hear, hear, hear." Over time, as you learn to increase your focus, the space between the words grows.

- **Don't get discouraged when you get distracted.** It happens to all of us. Every time you notice your mind drifting off into a thought or feeling, gently bring yourself back to your breath. Instead of getting frustrated with yourself for getting distracted, recognize yourself for noticing what your mind is doing. Every time you return to your breath, you're building your awareness and ability to focus, just as if you're building a muscle.

- **Experiment.** You have a lot of choices when it comes to starting a meditation practice, so feel free to experiment until you figure out what feels right for you. Try different types of meditation. Do you prefer guided or unguided meditation? Do you like sitting on the ground with your legs crossed, or is it better for you to sit a chair, or even lie down? Your preferences can change over time, but it's always good to start with what feels natural and easy.

- **Do it in baby steps.** Training your mind is the same as training your body. As with anything you want to change in your life, it's important to begin slowly. Start meditating for very short periods of time. Make the goal attainable. When you think about doing it, it should feel easy, not overwhelming. Meditate consistently for a period of time. When it starts to feel easy, increase the time incrementally.

- **Be consistent.** If you only go to the gym once a month, it's good for you, but it doesn't make much difference in your overall health. If you go a few times a week, however, you start to start to notice how much stronger and healthier you feel. Meditation works the same way. It's only worth doing if you do it consistently.

- **Put it on your schedule.** Treating meditation like an appointment makes it easier to be consistent about it. You're more likely to do it if you put it on your calendar and make it a priority. If you just promise yourself to meditate at some point, your negative mind will come up with a thousand reasons why there are more important things to do right now.

- **Try a class or a meet-up.** Meditating in a group with an instructor makes it easier to do longer sits, as well as to experiment with different techniques. Plus, it helps you create a schedule around your meditation practice.

HOW TO STICK WITH A MEDITATION PRACTICE

Once you start a meditation practice, the most challenging part can be to stay committed to it. It's a challenge to keep doing something that your negative mind resists. It can also be hard to process long-repressed emotions that might come up.

This is what happened to Diego. As he got deeper into his meditation practice, the childhood traumas he'd pushed into his subconscious started floating to the surface. He relived his sadness about his parents' divorce. To him, it felt like meditation was pulling him into a dark place. "I'm not getting anywhere," he told me. He wanted to quit.

Though I could understand why he wanted to stop, I wanted him to understand that the darkness was (unfortunately) a natural part of the process. What was happening to Diego is what happens to all of us when we decide to grow: the negative mind resists. It wants to keep us in survival mode. It doesn't want us to transform.

When you feel that pull from your negative mind, it's actually a sign that you're getting somewhere.

DOING IT IS WHAT MATTERS

If you're meditating regularly and find yourself constantly getting distracted, feeling frustrated, or descending into darkness, you're not alone. However, it's important to remind yourself that just the act of doing it is valuable.

As one of my meditation teachers once told me, "The goal is to accept everything you possibly can. All situations. All people, at all times. Including yourself." Try not to judge yourself for how you're meditating. Instead, think of the act itself as part of the growth process. The fact that you're putting energy and intention into accepting and improving yourself is what matters.

Here's another way to think about it: Every decision and action you take throughout the day is either moving you toward something positive or holding you back. Nothing is neutral. When you make the decision to meditate, you're making a decision to move toward something positive, regardless of what happens during that time.

Ultimately, Diego decided to stick with meditation, despite his growing pains. Little by little, as he continued with his practice, he learned to cope with his feelings of anxiety and depression. He did longer and longer sits. More and more, there were moments when he felt light and free.

In the meantime, his everyday life started to improve. He brushed up on cooking skills, and he found a job in the food industry. He made connections with people in his meditation group. He attended meditation retreats. He developed a vision for his future: building a tiny house and cooking for large groups of people.

Again, meditation isn't the only way to find calm and connect with your true self. When it comes to strengthening your coping mechanisms and creating the life you want, the goal is to find the path that works best for you. In the meantime, you can support the process of self-transformation—or even start the process—by taking care of your body.

PRACTICE

What baby steps can you take toward separating your true self from your negative mind?

Experiment with starting a meditation practice, using the steps we outlined in this chapter. Choose what feels challenging but doable for you, whether it's meditating for one minute every day, doing a ten-minute guided meditation, taking a meditation class, or going to yoga. Put your meditation activity on your calendar. Every time you do it, make note of it. Then take a moment to congratulate yourself for following through on your commitment to calming your mind. When you complete a streak—whether it's a week, two weeks, or forty days—reward yourself.

If you're not ready to meditate, or if you want to complement your meditation practice, think about the activities that help you connect with your true self. Which ones can you do daily? Which ones can you do less frequently? Put your true-self activities on your schedule just as you would with any other appointment. Start with the ones that feel the most powerful for you.

PART II

BODY AND MIND

CHAPTER 5

HOW TO BRING YOUR BODY INTO BALANCE

Growing up, I learned to associate food with joy. My dad is Italian, so we spent a lot of time in the kitchen. We cooked. We talked about recipes. Food was the way our family bonded.

Food was also how we rewarded ourselves. Whenever I accomplished something difficult, my mom took me out for ice cream. We didn't have things like ice cream or cake at our house, so eating sweets always felt exciting and special to me.

By the time I reached my twenties, I'd developed a huge attachment to food. I was addicted to cheeseburgers—every time I went snowboarding in Mammoth, I stopped at In-N-Out. Going out to dinner became one of my favorite things to do. I loved thinking about what I was going to order, especially when it came to dessert.

However, since I didn't want to gain weight, I always exercised. As long as I looked like I was in shape, I figured I was doing enough to take care of myself. In the meantime, though, I was drinking six Diet Cokes and smoking cigarettes every day.

Finally, at age twenty-nine, my immune system fell apart. Though I seemed to be thriving in every other aspect of my life—my emotional health, my psychotherapy practice, my friendships, my romantic life—I felt terrible physically. I was fighting sickness all the time, going from a cold to the flu and back again. I sought out doctors, but none of them could tell me what was wrong.

Finally I went to a naturopath doctor whose approach was more radical than the rest. He administered a series of blood tests, including an in-depth food intolerance test. He suggested I cut out all the foods my body couldn't tolerate: beef, beans, white fish, eggs, citrus fruit, gluten, and dairy products. On top of that, I had to give up alcohol, caffeine, and processed sugar.

The first few weeks were tough. Besides going through caffeine withdrawals, I was also adjusting mentally. I had to come to terms with my psychological attachment to food. My relationship with food—like everyone else's—was, and is, an emotional thing.

After I made it past the withdrawal phase, I couldn't believe how good I felt physically *and* psychologically. Aside from feeling sick so often, I thought I'd reached a high level of happiness and peace. However, after I eliminated the things that were bad for my body, I experienced a sense of total well-being I never thought possible.

By eating what my body wanted, I wasn't just helping it heal itself and function better, I was also helping my mind. I had no idea I could feel so clear-headed, calm, and fulfilled, much less that food could help me get there. Up to that point, I'd completely underestimated the power of my body and its impact on my mental health.

OUR BODIES FUEL OUR TRANSFORMATION

In some ways, it's obvious that your body affects how you feel. However, what I think most of us don't realize is *how much* your body influences your mind and emotions. I had to go to the extreme of completely changing my eating habits before I understood how powerful the mind-body connection really is.

I'm not saying you have to switch to a Paleo Autoimmune Protocol diet (AIP, a stricter version of the Paleo diet, which involves cutting out foods that cause inflammation in the digestive system by eating only meat, fish, and vegetables) in order to feel good. (Though this is what I ultimately did to strengthen my immune system.) What I am saying is that if you're not taking care of your physical body, it can be difficult to create the kind of transformation in your life that helps you become the best version of yourself.

There's an increasing amount of science that supports the connection between our bodies and our emotions, especially when it comes to diet. In a study published in the journal PLOS ONE, researchers found that diets high in processed foods increase inflammation, one of the risk factors for depression. Participants in the study who had the greatest increase in fruit and vegetable intake also showed the highest decrease in depression symptoms.[6]

In other words, what we eat can have a major impact on how we feel. At the same time, our emotions also affect the way our bodies function, especially when it comes to trauma. In *The Body Keeps the Score*, Bessel van der Kolk writes about the nature of trauma, how it gets stored in the body, and how it affects people physically as well as psychologically. When you go through something painful, it not only impacts your emotions but also your breathing and digestion. In fact, according to van der Kolk, it's very common that people who've experienced traumatic events in their lives also suffer from chronic digestive problems.

What does this mean? If you're using psychological and/or spiritual tools to work through your emotions, it's important to support this process by taking care of your body. Not only is your emotional health crucial to your physical health, but your physical health is crucial to your emotional health.

If you're not ready to cope with your emotions from a psychological or spiritual perspective, your body can be a place to start. In some cases, the body can even serve as a gateway to a larger healing process.

APPRECIATING YOUR BODY

Before we start exploring diet, exercise, and other alternatives for improving your physical health, I want to make

---

6   Heather M. Francis, Richard J. Stevenson, Jaime R. Chambers, Dolly Gupta, Brooklyn Newey, and Chai K. Lim, "A Brief Diet Intervention Can Reduce Symptoms of Depression in Young Adults," *PLOS One* 14, no. 10 (2019): e0222768. https://doi.org/10.1371/journal.pone.0222768

clear that this chapter is about learning to appreciate your body and its impact on your emotional health. It's not about achieving the "perfect body."

My goal is to empower you to see the connection between your physical health and your overall well-being. Seeing this connection starts with understanding that your value is not your body or your appearance.

Most of us understand this idea intellectually. However, it's often difficult to accept on an emotional level, since our media-driven culture is constantly sending us the opposite message.

When I'm trying to help clients develop an appreciation for their bodies, I start by asking them what they love most about the people close to them. It never has anything to do with their appearance. Instead, what they value in their relationships is how they connect with people on an emotional level.

So why does our appearance feel so important? Once again, it goes back to the survival mechanism in the negative mind. The better we look, the more likely we are to attract other people, especially people who want to mate with us, giving us a greater chance to reproduce and live longer.

Given that it's an instinctive response, it makes sense that we care so much about our appearance. So there's no reason to judge ourselves for caring about the way we look.

At the same time, it's important to go beyond our instincts and ask ourselves how much we're relying on our appearance to get other people to like us. Though it might seem like beautiful people have an easier time finding love, this is only true in the short term. Fulfilling, lasting relationships are based on who we are—not what we look like.

RECOGNIZE YOUR BEAUTY

Though it's important to understand that your value doesn't come from your physical appearance, it's just as important to learn to appreciate your own body.

For many people, this is difficult at first. It definitely was for my client Sophia, who was convinced that she was unattractive. Since she didn't fit into the media-cultural ideal of beauty, she didn't think anyone would be interested in her romantically. Her negative perception of her physical appearance affected how potential partners responded to her.

To help her change her internal programming, I asked Sophia to pause when she got out of the shower. Instead of looking in the mirror and picking out the things she hated about her body (as many of us do), I suggested she choose at least one body part she liked and focus on it for a minute.

"If you truly want to change your negative thought patterns around your body," I told her, "you have to put your conscious intention into it. It's not going to happen automatically."

Little by little, Sophia learned to appreciate her body for what it was. As her perceptions about herself changed, people started to respond to her differently. For the first time in her life, she felt confident. As we'll see in chapter

11, that confidence eventually led to a romantic relationship that's still going strong.

When you learn to honor your body in its current form, you develop the ability to feel confident, no matter how your appearance changes. On the other hand, if you tell yourself you need to reach a certain weight or fix a certain feature before you can feel good, you'll never be satisfied.

If you lose ten pounds, for example, you'll have a window of time where you feel confident about your body. Before long, though, your mind will go back to picking out something else you don't like. Why? Again, because it's the mind's job to look for what's wrong in any given situation, and to keep you in an anxious state, especially when it comes to your appearance.

In order to rewrite your negative programming around your body, you have to consistently practice appreciating your physical self—even though it might go against your instincts. However, as with anything you practice, it gets easier over time.

APPRECIATE HOW YOUR BODY WORKS FOR YOU

Besides learning to appreciate your body for what it is, it's also important to acknowledge how it allows you to function. For example, when my immune system is working well, I make a point to say something like, "Thanks for being strong and working this out."

Why is this important? By directing gratitude and love inward, I create a positive momentum loop. Instead of regretting what my body can't do, and getting caught up in my physical limitations, I acknowledge what my body is capable of, which supports its ability to heal. Remember, as I wrote at the top of this chapter, our emotions affect our bodies just as much as our bodies affect our emotions.

Even when I'm not feeling well, I thank my body for giving me the ability to exercise, do my job, and think clearly. I think about the things in my life that make me feel fulfilled.

I recognize that I'm able to do both of those things by saying, "Thank you, physical body, for allowing me to walk. Thank you for giving me the ability to still connect with the people I care about."

HOW TO IMPROVE YOUR RELATIONSHIP WITH FOOD

As I wrote at the beginning of this chapter, many of us, including me, associate food with joy. However, when you take a closer look at your attachment to food, it can open up a whole new pathway to controlling your own happiness. In other words, being honest about your relationship with food makes it easier to release the resistance to changing that relationship. Besides that, when you stop judging your-self for your eating habits, you create the psychological space to make new choices around them.

In her book *Women, Food and God*, Geneen Roth explains how we use food to leave our bodies or avoid emotional experiences. When we feel anxious or stressed, for exam-ple, we often crave things like chocolate or cheeseburgers. Instead of facing our emotions head-on, we tend to sidestep them by "rewarding" ourselves with food.

As someone who struggled with her weight, Roth wanted to be more conscious about the ways she used food to self-soothe. She also wanted to find a way to improve her relationship with food without feeling like she was depriving herself.

The first thing she discovered was that she needed to stop herself from eating unconsciously. She didn't change anything about what she was eating. She just sat with her food, chewing it, tasting it, and seeing what was happening for her. Did she feel like she had to eat as quickly as possible? Was it hard for her to sit still while she ate? What did she think that food was giving her?

If she felt like a particular food was making her happy, she asked herself whether that was actually true. And if it was true, how long did that happiness last?

In Roth's experience, changing your relationship with food isn't about restricting yourself. It's about learning to relate to food in a conscious way. You can eat whatever you want. The key is to pay attention while you're doing it. If you're not sure how, here are Roth's seven rules for creating mindfulness around food:

1. Eat when you're hungry

2. Eat sitting down in a calm environment

3. Eat without distractions (no reading, no driving, no surfing the Internet or watching TV)

4. Eat what your body wants

5. Eat with gusto, enjoyment, and pleasure

6. Eat until you're satisfied

7. Eat (with the intention of) being in full view of others

If you make a point to eat mindfully, you automatically start to break down your unconscious patterns around food. Noting your eating habits helps you see how they're connected to your emotions.

For example, when I noticed myself feeling fulfilled and happy when I ate dessert, I realized I associated sweets with connecting to my mom. Wasn't there another way I could create that sense of connection with her? Why not text her? Or invite her to a tea bar?

Now that I knew the dessert wasn't actually creating that connection with my mom, the key was to find a way to give myself the feeling I *thought* the dessert was giving me.

THE TWO PARTS OF BUILDING HEALTHY EATING HABITS

While it's important to deconstruct your relationship with food, it's just as important to take action toward creating healthy eating habits.

In other words, if you want to improve your relationship with food, the key is to approach it in two ways:

1. Evaluate your connections and associations with food and look at your family's history around eating.

2. Make a plan and take baby steps toward your goals.

When I work with clients who want to address their relationship with food, I always ask them a series of questions:

- How would you describe your family's relationship with food? Did you cook together? Did you sit down together at dinnertime? Did you celebrate with food?

- Are there specific foods that you connect with certain emotions? (For example, did your parents give you sweets after you made it through something difficult?)

- Do you reward yourself with food?

- Do you use food to cope with stress? How?

- What's the hardest time of the day to eat healthy or not binge?

- Where do you feel like you're messing up the most? Is it the amount of food in your body? Is it the type of food you're putting in your body?

- How far in advance do you plan your meals? Do you wait until the last minute to figure out what to eat?

- What would you like to change about your relationship with food?

Once you figure out where your challenges are, start with baby steps (an idea we'll explore in more detail toward the end of this chapter).

For example, you could start by limiting yourself to three meals a day but choosing what to eat at those meals. Or if you're someone who needs to snack, start by eating healthier snacks.

If you eat three poor meals a day, which one would be the easiest to make healthier? For many people, that's breakfast. If you want to eat junk food at lunch and dinner, go ahead. Then, when eating a healthy breakfast starts to feel easy, add another meal to the healthy category.

When you're looking for an approach to food that feels right, the key is to ask yourself where your problem areas are—then decide on the easiest way to tweak them.

WHY EXERCISE?

Earlier in this chapter I mentioned the fact that emotions get stored in our bodies. If you want to feel better psychologically as well as physically, besides paying attention to what you're eating, it's important to move at least a little bit every day.

There are numerous scientific studies that make the correlation between physical activity and emotional health. According to a study published by the American College of Sports Medicine, doing cardiovascular exercise for thirty minutes a day, four days a week is the chemical equivalent of taking an anti-depressant.[7] So it's no surprise that more and more therapists are incorporating body awareness and movement into their work with clients.

---

7   James A. Blumenthal, Patrick J. Smith, and Benson M. Hoffman, "Is Exercise a Viable Treatment for Depression?" ACSMs Health & Fitness Journal 16, no. 4 (2012): 14-21

Getting your heart rate up is a game-changer in terms of releasing stagnant feelings. As someone who moves their body five or six days a week, I speak from experience. If I don't exercise, I can feel the emotions build up in my body, especially since I have an emotional job.

For some of my clients, exercise is the easiest place to start releasing their emotions. For others, it's a real challenge, especially if they didn't grow up exercising in their family or if they were conditioned to think of working out as being torturous.

The truth is we all resist exercise to some degree. Again, that resistance goes back to the survival instincts in the negative mind, which are telling you the best way to stay alive is to conserve your energy and do as little as possible. Your mind is still running that program, even though most of us hardly have to move in our modern lives.

My dad likes to say, "Have you ever left the gym and regretted it?" Of course my answer is always "no." You can count on your negative mind to insist that you sit still. But when you realize what a difference it can make in how you feel, it becomes easier and easier to motivate yourself.

OTHER WAYS TO MOVE ENERGY

If you have physical problems that keep you from exercising, enlist other people to help you move your energy. For example, massage and acupuncture are non-invasive options I always suggest to clients who want to release the tension and clear the stagnation in their bodies.

If you can't afford massage or acupuncture, try researching massage or Chinese medicine schools in your area. Students at these schools are required to complete a certain number of training hours, and they frequently offer free or low-cost treatments.

BREAKING THROUGH RESISTANCE

Even when you know certain things are good for you, sometimes it's hard to motivate yourself to make healthy choices. Why?

Again, it goes back to the negative mind. As I wrote in chapter 1, the negative mind is rooted in your survival instinct. So it's telling you to preserve your energy as much as possible by sitting still and taking in as many calories as you can.

The negative mind isn't designed for our sedentary way of life. It dates back to a time when we were moving around all the time and needed to rest and eat as much as we could in order to recuperate.

What does this mean? Your mind will resist when you decide to do things like exercise or change your eating habits. However, just being aware of where that resistance is coming from makes it easier to move beyond it.

BABY STEPS

As Darren Hardy writes in *The Compound Effect*,[8] the tiny decisions you make over time can add up to huge changes in your life. When you learn to break things down into manageable, bite-sized pieces, you make it easier to keep moving toward your goals.

Hardy tells the story of Scott, Brad, and Larry—three friends on similar life paths—to illustrate how seemingly small choices end up having a long-term impact. All three were married, living in the same neighborhood, and earning approximately $50,000 a year. They were all at a relatively healthy body weight. Over a three year period, Scott, Brad, and Larry made very different everyday choices that eventually changed the course of their lives.

While Brad bought a big-screen TV and increased his daily alcohol consumption, Larry made no changes to his lifestyle. In the meantime, Scott decided to trade his favorite soda for water, which cut 125 calories from his diet every day. Besides that, Scott made a daily commitment to read ten pages of self-development books and take a thirty-minute walk.

After five months, the differences between the three friends were not dramatic. However, after two years, the contrast was astonishing. Scott lost thirty-three pounds. After investing almost a thousand hours in self-improvement research, he earned a promotion and a raise at his job. His marriage was thriving.

---

8   Darren Hardy, *The Compound Effect* (New York: Vanguard Press, 2010).

In the meantime, Brad wasn't doing well. Besides gaining over thirty pounds, he was struggling in his marriage, withdrawing from his wife, and continuing to turn to food and television as a source of comfort. Larry's situation didn't change much, except that he'd grown bitter about the government and complained about paying high taxes.

The story of Scott, Brad, and Larry shows us how small steps can lead to big results. Whether it's anxiety, depression, or your diet, the key to transforming it isn't to do everything all at once (as tempting as it might be). Instead, the way to transformation is to find the easiest point of entry—the smallest, most reasonable action you can take—and start there.

As I wrote in the Introduction, when I decided to take better care of my body, I didn't go straight from smoking, eating cheeseburgers, and drinking Diet Coke to a strict Paleo diet—it took me years to make the switch. Along the way, I took baby steps, like ordering dinner salads. I'd still have a cheeseburger and fries, but I made myself eat a salad first. Sometimes the salad would fill me up, and I'd eat less of the rest of my meal. But I still had everything I wanted on my plate.

I wasn't ready to give up the cheeseburgers and fries—yet.

GIVE YOURSELF CREDIT

It's easy to undervalue your effort when you take a baby step toward your goal. However, if you don't give yourself credit, there's no motivation to go through the experience again. It may seem unnatural at first, but you want to get to a point where you celebrate every step you take, even if it's "just" ordering a dinner salad.

It's not about the size of the step you take. It's about learning to acknowledge yourself for taking a step in the first place.

Though your negative mind is always going to look for the next place to go, it's important to pause and appreciate what's happening in the moment. In other words, you want to create a positive momentum loop.

Most of us are used to being in a negative momentum loop, where we take a step in a positive direction but don't acknowledge ourselves for taking that step. For example, when we make a healthy choice, like skipping dessert or substituting water for soda, instead of taking the time to reward ourselves, we often think about the next step we need to take, or we tell ourselves it's no big deal.

However, when you don't take the time to recognize yourself for making smart choices, two things happen: one, you miss out on the dessert, the soda, or whatever it is you're skipping, and, two, you take away an opportunity to feel fulfilled for doing something good for your health.

On the other hand, when you learn to recognize yourself for each step you take, it not only becomes easier to reach your goals, it also helps you enjoy the journey. When I was trying to eat healthier, I made it a point every night to acknowledge myself for what I'd accomplished that day. If I'd eaten a salad with my fast-food dinner, for example, I'd tell myself: "Great job, Jesse! You ate fewer fries and more salad today."

Feeling good about myself motivated me to keep putting one foot in front of the other. Over time, as the power of my positive momentum loop expanded, I was inspired to take bigger and bigger steps.

After a month of eating dinner salads, for example, I decided to wrap my burger in lettuce. Sometimes I had a salad with chicken and a side of fries; other times it was a salad and a burger. Eventually, I decided to swap a cheeseburger for a salad. When I noticed how different I felt after eating a salad for lunch instead of a cheeseburger and fries, it continued to feed my motivation. My body actually started to crave healthier foods. Over time, it became easier to make smarter choices and take bigger steps toward eating better.

As a result, by the time I met the doctor who recommended the Paleo autoimmune protocol (AIP) diet, I was ready for his plan, even though it was a huge change.

Had I met that doctor five years earlier—i.e., had I not taken all those small steps leading to this larger one—I doubt I could have committed to such a strict diet. However, I'd spent years creating a positive momentum loop around my eating habits and noticing how much better I felt emotionally and psychologically as I made healthier food choices. So in the end, the amount of effort it took to take this giant step was the same amount of effort it took to take the initial baby step of adding a dinner salad to my diet.

HOW TO COMMIT TO A HEALTHY ROUTINE

Even when you overcome your initial resistance to establishing healthy habits, it can be a challenge to stick with them over time. Feeling the effects of your effort takes work. It also takes time and consistency.

When my clients want to shift to a healthier routine, along with taking baby steps and rewarding themselves afterward, these are the strategies that help them stay committed:

1. **Make it fun.** When it comes to exercise, experiment with different ways of moving your body until you find things you genuinely look forward to, like going for a walk outside, taking classes with that hilarious aerobics teacher at the gym, or ice skating at the local rink. With food, try bringing some humor into it. When my mom and I decided to take a month-long break from dessert, we texted each other pictures of all the desserts we were turning down everywhere we went. "Look at this beautiful cake I'm not eating!" I wrote her. "Check out these donuts I just said 'no' to!" she wrote back. We made it a kind of competition, which made it more fun.

2. **Mix it up.** Not only is it important to move the energy in your body, but it's also important to move that energy in different ways. Try yoga. Try running. Make a playlist and dance to it. Experiment with different types of breathing, too. If you get stuck in a routine, your body will adapt to that routine, making it more challenging to release whatever emotions you're holding on to. Besides that, mixing up your routine makes exercising more fun, which makes it easier for you to stay motivated. The same goes for food. If you're having trouble coming up with ways to vary your diet, schedule an hour to go online (or read cookbooks) and look for recipes that sound exciting to you. Pick a new vegetable to try

every week. There will be times when other things have priority in your life, but it's important to rotate the foods you eat as much as you can.

3. **Do it with a friend.** Instead of going to a bar and having a drink, how about exercising or cooking with a friend? Not only are you socializing, but you're also doing something that makes you feel good afterward. Plus, doing things with a friend is an easy way to hold yourself accountable.

4. **Tell a friend.** If you can't find a friend to exercise or eat with, ask someone to hold you accountable. When I want to make sure I follow through on taking care of myself, I have my friend Zoë check up on me. "Hey, Zoë, will you ask me tomorrow if I went to Pilates?" Knowing she's going to ask me about it increases my motivation to go.

5. **Schedule it.** In chapter 4, I brought up the idea of scheduling meditation to help you stick with it. The same goes for taking care of your body. If you're having trouble motivating yourself to exercise, write it in your schedule like any other appointment. You're much more likely to do it if it's on your calendar.

6. **Create goals, breaking them down into baby steps.** Every day, every week, every month, and every quarter, take time to think about what your intentions are for your body. For example, maybe your goal for the next month is variety of exercise. Each week, choose a different class or activity. Keep your goals challenging but doable.

7. **Write down your goals.** According to a study at Dominican University,[9] you're forty-two percent more likely to accomplish your goals if you write them down. Why? Besides helping you get clear about what you want to do, writing down your goals also pushes you to assess your progress and come up with strategies for success.

8. **Look for the joy in your pain.** When I'm walking up a hill in high altitude, when my muscles are screaming and I'm out of breath, my negative mind automatically starts telling me to stop and turn around. Even though I'm hearing that voice, I try to think past it. How? By looking for the pleasure in the difficulty: "Wow, this is hard," I tell myself, "And I'm going to do it anyway. And it's going to feel great when I make it to the top." The next time I'm facing a difficult situation, I can draw on the memory of hiking to the top of that hill. And I can remind myself how amazing I felt when I got to the top. As I mentioned in chapter 1, accomplishing something challenging helps you bring meaning and purpose into your life. And the more meaning and purpose you can bring into your life, the easier it is to cope with feelings of doubt and emptiness—and find the strength to persevere when it's tempting to give up.

9. **Be kind to yourself when you fall off the wagon.** The number one reason diets (or any healthy, growth-related routine) fail is because people try to do everything at once. Instead of taking a baby step, they start with a

---

9   Peter Economy. "This is the Way You Need to Write Down Your Goals for Faster Success." Inc. com. inc.com/peter-economy/this-is-the-way-you-need-to-write-down-your-goals-for-faster-success (accessed December 19, 2019)

huge, impossible goal and then feel down on themselves when they can't follow through with it.

However, even if you're taking the baby-step approach toward your goals, you're going to stumble and fall at some point. In fact, falling off the wagon is part of the process. As much as we'd like to think growth happens in a straight, forward-moving line, the truth is that it's always three steps forward, two steps back.

So when you fall off the wagon, don't get angry with yourself. Instead, show yourself some love, as you would with anyone you care about.

When you fall off the wagon, the key is to shorten the amount of time it takes you to get back on. It's not about keeping yourself from falling off in the first place. Falling off just means you're going after a challenge—and you deserve credit for that.

If any of these steps seem overwhelming or impossible to you right now, I have some good news for you: it gets easier. The more consistently you do good things for your body, the more your body will start to crave them.

Though it took years—and many, many baby steps—before I arrived at the point where I wanted vegetables more than Diet Coke, I got here. Whether you're trying to adopt a healthy routine or give up habits that are knocking you off balance, I know you can get here, too.

PRACTICE

Rate your relationship with your body on a scale from one to ten, one being you hate your body, and ten being you feel beautiful, healthy, and happy all the time. If you come down toward the lower end of the scale, what do you need to do in order to change your feelings around your body?

If you feel that your eating habits are the source of your negative feelings around your body, think about the baby steps you could take to improve your relationship with food. For example, commit to eating when you're hungry, when you're sitting down, when you're not distracted—or commit to eating one healthy meal a day.

If the fact that you're not exercising enough and is the source of your negative feelings around your body, then think about the baby steps you can take to move your body on a regular basis. Is it taking a ten-minute walk after dinner? Playing with your dog for fifteen minutes a day? Riding your bike to work once or twice a week?

Think about what you need to do in order to integrate these healthy habits into your life. For example, do you need to put your phone in another room when you're eating? Or wake up earlier to give yourself time to bike to work? Track your progress daily and reward yourself every time you take a baby step.

After a month, evaluate your progress. If you've been consistently following through on your baby steps, it's time to celebrate. For example, treat yourself to a massage, or a new piece of clothing. Get your hair blow-dried or splurge on a smoothie or a meal at your favorite healthy restaurant.

If you feel stuck after a month, then your steps were too big; go back and make them smaller. If at that point it still feels too difficult to create a healthy routine on your own, find an accountability partner who can help you stay committed to your goals.

CHAPTER 6

HOW TO DEAL WITH ALCOHOL AND DRUGS

The first time Ben came to my office for therapy, it seemed like there was a war going on inside him. "I want to be a firefighter, and I want to be a good father to my son," he told me. "I also want to stop drinking."

When he was thirteen, Ben's father caused a drunk-driving accident that left him mentally handicapped for life. After that, Ben started drinking himself, often to the point where he would blackout or get into fights.

Getting drunk and losing control became a way to deal with his grief. Meanwhile, Ben's relationship with his mother, who raised Ben and his three brothers on her own, deteriorated. She constantly yelled at Ben, telling him how awful, unhelpful, and manipulative he was.

At seventeen, Ben became a father. Unlike his own dad,

he decided he wanted to be present for his son. He vowed not to put him through the trauma his father had put him through. However, given his relationship with alcohol, he didn't hold much hope for himself.

Without alcohol, Ben couldn't imagine being able to have fun and connect with his friends. On top of that, his mind was anxious. Though he came across like an alpha male with a great sense of humor, he was a sensitive person who felt things deeply.

Over time, he'd internalized his mother's words: He was a terrible person. He was rude, selfish, and inconsiderate. Drinking was the only way he knew to quiet his mind and stop feeling bad about himself.

"I want to be a better person," he told me. "But it's not in my control yet. I drink. Then I drink too much, and then I make a mess."

Ben tried to cope without alcohol for a while. He read self-help books. He went to church. He moved closer to his dream of getting a job in the fire department. Then he got arrested for driving under the influence, and things fell apart.

WE'RE ALL ON A CONTINUUM

Are you or aren't you an addict? Like Ben, sometimes we think we have to label ourselves as one or the other. Either you are an alcoholic or you're not. Either you need drugs to cope or you do them recreationally.

However, it's far more helpful to look at your relationship

with alcohol and drugs on a continuum. Evaluate it on a scale of one to ten, one being "I'm just using alcohol to have an interesting, different mental experience," and ten being "I can't function without it."

Most of us are somewhere toward the middle of this scale. The truth is that there's no clear line between people who use alcohol and drugs for fun and people who need them to cope. If you're using them in any form, you're altering your mind. You're getting something from them. And that's okay. The important thing is to be aware of the degree to which you're relying on them, as well as understand what they're giving you.

START WITH ACCEPTANCE

When you're evaluating your relationship with alcohol and drugs, it's important to start from a place of acceptance.

Accepting your relationship with alcohol and drugs doesn't mean you'll be stuck in that relationship. Giving yourself empathy doesn't tie to you those substances. Instead, it starts to free you from them. How does this work?

As with anxiety and depression, what often stops us from changing an emotion or a behavior is the feeling about the feeling, or the feeling about the behavior. For example, in my family, drinking was how we had fun and connected to each other. When I started drinking in my twenties, alcohol made it easier for me to overcome my shyness—especially at large social gatherings or in situations with people I didn't know. Though I usually only had two drinks, I still judged myself for depending on alcohol to have a good time.

However, once I realized how I was using alcohol, and recognized what it was giving me, I learned to accept my relationship with it instead of judging myself for it. After that, I could choose whether and how I wanted to change that relationship.

As I mentioned in chapter 5, once you can be honest about your relationship with the substances in your life (which include food as well as alcohol and drugs) you can let go of the resistance to changing that relationship. When you stop judging yourself, it becomes easier to make a new choice.

This is why Alcoholics Anonymous (AA) works so well. Just the act of sitting with a group of people who accept their relationship with alcohol, even though it's made them do horrible things, helps release the stronghold of the addiction. Instead of continuing to tell themselves how awful and worthless they are (which drove them to drink in the first place), members of AA learn to develop an understanding of the reasons behind their relationship with alcohol, which in turn allows them to take responsibility for their actions. This is when healing begins.

WHY DO WE TURN TO ALCOHOL AND DRUGS?

As we transition out of childhood, there are different reasons we turn to alcohol and drugs. Like Ben, some of us learn to use substances (in varying degrees) to numb our pain or distract ourselves from reality. Some of us become dependent on things like alcohol to tamp down our inhibitions, boost our confidence, and/or have a good time. Some of us use drugs, from meth and cocaine to tobacco or caffeine, to raise our energy level or enhance our focus.

Some of us smoke pot or take psychedelics in order to reach a spiritual place.

In the end, though, we turn to substances for two reasons: to avoid the bad and bring out the good. In other words, we use substances to protect ourselves against emotions we don't want to feel, instead of allowing ourselves to experience feelings like sadness or fear. We also depend on substances to tap into happiness and feelings of fulfillment.

Why does this matter? Ultimately, if you're using anything on a regular basis to avoid your feelings or access parts of yourself you can't reach when you're sober, you're not building your coping skills.

Even if you're able to function, when you depend on a substance to make it through the day, or wait for the weekend to go on a drinking binge (like Ben did), you're basically fast-forwarding past emotions like sadness, fear, and anger without learning how to handle them. Over time, these emotions build up and get stuck. So does the pain.

As I wrote in the introduction, in the process of self-transformation, what you resist will persist—and what you accept will transform. Redefining your relationship with the substances in your life starts with asking yourself what those substances are giving you.

Once you understand what you're getting from the substances in your life, you can experiment with ways to create those feelings or experiences without them. This is one of the keys to becoming the best version of yourself.

Later in this chapter, we'll explore ways to create a healthy relationship with alcohol and drugs. We'll also weigh the idea of moderation versus abstinence, and how to determine which approach is right for you.

First, let's take a look at the most common substances we use, focusing on how they impact us emotionally and physically.

ALCOHOL

Many of us think we're a more attractive version of ourselves when we drink. After having a cocktail, we start to let go of our inhibitions. Like Ben, we feel freer, lighter, and funnier. It's easier to talk with people.

In my twenties, I didn't have the confidence to be at a party or a large social gathering without drinking. As an introvert, it was hard for me to talk with people I didn't know and share things about myself; I usually felt anxious until I had my first drink in my hand. Again, though I only had a couple of drinks, I'd programmed myself to think I needed them to take the edge off: "Once I have this cocktail," I'd tell myself, "I'll be relaxed."

Of course, that sense of relaxation was temporary. Why? Alcohol is a depressant. Even though you may not feel it when you drink, the depressive component usually kicks in the days *after* you drink, lowering your mood and making you more depressed and/or anxious.

For example, my client Caroline liked to spend weekends drinking with her friends. During the week, she didn't have more than a glass of wine here and there. So she didn't understand why she was having panic attacks during the week, especially on Thursday nights.

When I suggested that there might be a connection between the alcohol and her panic attacks, she didn't believe me at first. "I don't think it's affecting me like that," she said. "It's happening five days after I drink."

Drinking with her friends was the highlight of her week, and Caroline wasn't ready to give it up. But her panic attacks persisted. Eventually, though she was still skeptical, she decided to experiment with giving up alcohol for a month. After two weeks, her panic attacks stopped.

Alcohol can also affect some of us in more subtle ways. Though everyone's body chemistry is different, the fact is that alcohol stays in our bodies and lowers our mood, turning up the volume on our negative mind.

Depending on what our emotional triggers are, the depressive effects of alcohol can bring up thoughts of self-doubt and self-deprecation, depression, anxiety and/or panic attacks—even days after we drink.

MARIJUANA

Although I support the movement toward legalizing marijuana, especially for people who use it for medical purposes, I think we underestimate the effects of pot. For one thing, most of the marijuana people use today is much more potent than what was available in the 1970s.

According to a University of Mississippi study that measured tetrahydrocannabinol (THC) levels in 39,000 samples of marijuana over a twenty-year period, the THC content in the samples increased from four percent in 1995 to approximately twelve percent in 2014. Why does this matter? THC is the main psychoactive ingredient in marijuana. Smoking marijuana with lower doses of THC creates "a pleasant feeling; [giving you] the munchies, the happiness," said lead study author Mahmoud A. ElSohly. However, ElSohly added that using marijuana with high THC levels creates a higher risk of negative side effects like psychosis or panic attacks.[10]

I know from my own experience that smoking pot on a daily basis can be a motivation killer. In my early twenties, I smoked every night before I went to sleep. After surviving a home invasion when I was twelve years old, I always felt anxious going to sleep at night. I didn't like being in a pitch-black room. I never forgot the image of that man standing in my bedroom doorway. After that, I slept as far away from doorways as possible.

When I discovered pot, I thought, "Great! Now I have something to block out that image and help me sleep." What I didn't realize was that the pot was preventing me from working through my trauma.

After a few years of smoking every night, I went to a meditation retreat, where I had an epiphany. As I wrote in the introduction, I'd thought of myself as an analytical person up to that point. I liked working through things in my mind.

---

10 Agata Blaszczak-Boxe. "Potent Pot: Marijuana Is Stronger Now Than It Was 20 Years Ago." LiveScience.com. February 9, 2016. Accessed January 20, 2020. https://www.livescience.com/amp/53644-marijuana-is-stronger-now-than-20-years-ago.html.

But something shifted inside me at that retreat: for weeks afterward, I felt as peaceful and joyful as I felt when I smoked pot. "It's actually possible to have this feeling without using substances?" I thought. "That's my new goal."

Initially, giving up pot was difficult, even though I was taking baby steps. I had a hard time going to sleep at night. Over time, though, I started to notice positive changes. My memory improved. My energy level went up. It felt easier to go after my goals, both on a small and a large scale. I read more, I ate better, and I was more motivated to exercise. It became easier to connect with people, too. Ultimately, I felt more alive.

PSYCHEDELICS

As a therapist, I'm glad on one level that psychedelics are becoming an avenue for people to open their minds to feel and see things differently. For relatively psychologically stable people who are facing existential stressors like cancer, for example, psychedelics can be a great source of healing.

On the other hand, I think it's problematic to treat psychedelics as a quick fix, especially for people in a chronic, psychologically fragile state. As psychedelics become popular, more and more people are turning to things like micro-dosing and ayahuasca, instead of doing the work to transform their negative emotions.

Don't get me wrong: I'm not saying you can't gain important insights and have eye-opening experiences with psychedelics. As I tell my clients, there is no right and wrong when it comes to finding ways to heal your psychological problems. However, I think it's dangerous to think that you can transform yourself, or learn to cope with anxiety or depression, without doing the emotional work (which we explored in chapters 1 through 3)—and without being centered in reality.

For example, my client Emma, who suffered from severe depression and anxiety, turned to ayahuasca early on in our sessions together. Since she was so psychologically fragile, I worried about her using psychedelics. Instead of helping her see things more clearly, ayahuasca had the potential to fragment her mind and make her lose touch with reality.

Though she didn't have a psychotic episode, Emma felt more depressed and anxious than ever after the ayahuasca ceremony. Why? Exposing herself to the truth didn't give her the coping skills to deal with it. The insights themselves weren't enough—afterward, she had to do the emotional work around them.

CAFFEINE, NICOTINE, AND OTHER STIMULANTS

Stimulants like nicotine and caffeine usually start out feeling fun and pleasurable. After all, they boost our energy and help us focus, right?

However, as you probably know from your own experience, the effects of cigarettes (or vaping) and caffeine don't last. The more you use them, the more your body loses the capacity to naturally energize itself.

"I'm so tired in the morning," my clients tell me. "I could never give up caffeine!" What I want them to understand is that the caffeine and other stimulants actually create the problem they're trying to solve.

Your body is designed to wake up naturally and give you energy throughout the day. When you interrupt that process with coffee, cigarettes, and/or other stimulants, you're disconnecting from your natural energy.

If you're feeling tired all the time and using stimulants to push through your fatigue, you're basically telling your body to stop producing its own energy.

Besides lowering your natural energy level, caffeine and other stimulants can cause low-grade anxiety. Every time I've lowered my caffeine intake, I've noticed how relaxed, centered, and balanced I've felt. A lot of my clients tell me, "Oh, no, caffeine doesn't really make me anxious." But you can't know for sure until you give it up.

Whether you're having one cup of coffee or a hundred cigarettes a day, your body will adjust accordingly. The key to increasing your energy level over time, and gauging whether stimulants might be making you anxious, is to experiment with moderating or gradually letting go of them.

> If you're thinking about quitting coffee or caffeine, know that it takes more than a few days or a week for your body to adjust. Though the withdrawal headaches usually diminish after a couple of days, you might still feel sluggish and foggy-headed. In most cases, your body will need about a month to shift into producing its own energy. The bottom line: give it time. You won't know how it feels to let go of caffeine unless you allow your body enough time to adapt.

HOW TO REDEFINE YOUR RELATIONSHIP WITH ALCOHOL AND DRUGS

How do you know when you want to quit using a substance altogether versus using it in moderation? Start by asking yourself what void the substance(s) is filling. What is it giving you? How are you using it to cope?

If you're having trouble answering these questions, ask yourself what role the substance(s) played in your family.

Every family has its own culture around alcohol, for example. Did no one in your family drink? Did people drink until they were out of control? Ben, whose story opens this chapter, grew up in a home where you couldn't have fun if you weren't drinking. So he learned to associate sobriety with boredom, awkwardness, and sadness.

Your relationship with alcohol and drugs is always adaptive. It's something you learn as you grow up. It's no coincidence, for example, that I smoked cigarettes for ten years. All of my older cousins smoked cigarettes. As an only child, I learned to connect the smell of cigarettes with the feeling of being close and having siblings. After my cousins committed suicide, I started smoking. Smoking was my way of bonding with them.

CONSIDER ABSTINENCE

As I wrote at the top of this chapter, you're not an addict, and you're not dysfunctional, if you use drugs or alcohol. Again, though, if you do use them, you're most likely using them to cope in some way, whether it's to avoid negative emotions or tap into positive ones.

When I share this idea with clients, most of them resist. They say things like, "Well, I don't think I'm using X to cope. I mean, I don't *need* it."

Again, you don't know how a substance is affecting your emotional experience, or what function it's serving in your life, unless you give it up, at least in the short-term. The more you resist this idea, the more likely it is that you're relying on it to function.

As I tell my clients, if you're truly committed to finding clarity in your relationship with alcohol and drugs—and truly committing to becoming the best version of yourself—you need to give them up entirely for a set period of time. Even if you're nowhere close to having a problem with the substances in your life, you can still get massive benefits from abstaining from them for a while.

TREAT IT LIKE AN EXPERIMENT

See what happens when you abstain from alcohol and drugs for thirty days. If thirty days sounds impossible, try one or two weeks. If a period of one or two weeks isn't doable for you, try cutting back. For example, I tell daily pot smokers to see how late in the day they can wait to start smoking. (Can they make it until after work?) For people who drink every day, we start out by reducing the number of drinks they have each day, or we experiment with them only drinking on the weekends.

Regardless of how much time you decide to go without your chosen substance, when you commit to a period of abstinence, it helps you evaluate what you're getting from alcohol and drugs, and how you're using them to cope.

In the meantime, you're also creating space to feel your feelings, instead of using a substance to numb them. For many of my clients, this can be the most challenging aspect of an experiment with abstinence. Keeping a journal helps. Writing about your emotions helps release the negative mind's resistance to the experiment.

For example, when I quit smoking, I felt things much more intensely. After just a few days without cigarettes, I realized I'd been lighting up every time I had an intense emotion—positive or negative. Taking away the ritual of the cigarettes forced me to be more present in my feelings—and journaling helped me process those feelings.

Once you've written a few lines in your journal and/or spent a few minutes reflecting on your emotions, give yourself permission to distract. As I wrote in chapter 3, after an intense period of diving into your feelings, it helps to give yourself a break from them. Watch a movie. Go for a walk. Fix yourself something healthy to eat. Anything that lowers the volume on your negative mind is going to help you continue to take those baby steps forward.

Speaking of baby steps, it's important to celebrate each one you take in your abstinence experiment. As I've written throughout this book, giving yourself positive reinforcement is the key to staying motivated on the path to self-transformation. Instead of focusing on how deprived you feel without alcohol and drugs, tell yourself how amazing you are for having made it this far: "Hey, Self! You've made it three days without a drink. You rock!"

AFTER YOUR EXPERIMENT, REFLECT

Once you complete your abstinence experiment, take some time to reflect. Think about your unconscious beliefs around alcohol and drugs. Does alcohol make you feel more confident or free from pain? Does smoking make you feel cool and give you a sense of belonging? Does pot take you to a spiritual place?

Once you're clear about your beliefs around alcohol and drugs, ask yourself if there's another way to get what they're giving you. How can you develop confidence, and/or find comfort, without alcohol? How can you relax and feel connected to people besides smoking? How can you tap into your spiritual side without doing pot?

Of course, once you give up alcohol or drugs, it takes time to develop the parts of yourself that the substance has been helping you cope with. Though we live in an age when things move incredibly quickly, and we're used to instant solutions and gratification, it's important to remember that real, lasting transformation takes time and effort. You won't automatically become confident, centered, and secure after you give up your chosen substance—but I promise you will if you stick with it.

EXPERIMENT WITH MODERATION

After you finish your abstinence experiment, experiment with gradually bringing that substance back into your life. Do you notice a difference? How does it feel? Are you still creating negative experiences around that substance? How do you feel physically after you use it? How do you feel emotionally? Do you wake up the next day and feel a little more anxious or depressed?

If the substance continues to have a negative impact on your mind and body, abstinence might be the best choice.

How do you know for sure? If you have one drink, is it enough for you? Or do you obsess about it to the point where you have to have another? If you have a cup of coffee in the afternoon, do you feel more anxious or have trouble sleeping?

In other words, do you feel like you have control over your choices without depriving yourself?

Again, the key here is to experiment. After you commit to an initial period of time without your chosen substance[11], try both moderation and abstinence. In each case, take the time to note how your body and mind react. You'll be able to feel which approach makes sense for you right now.

WHEN YOU WANT TO QUIT

The only way out of an addiction is through. If you decide you're ready to quit something, know that the first stage can feel especially intense. When Ben was trying to give up alcohol, he came face to face with his feelings of anxiety. When he wasn't drinking, those feelings became stronger.

Though he could glimpse the person he wanted to be, all

---

11   It's important to choose one substance at a time to experiment with. I don't recommend experimenting with multiple substances at once because it makes it easier to fail, or give up. As with anything you want to change in your life, taking baby steps is the key to maintaining your forward momentum.

of the programming and trauma he went through when he was younger made it hard to hold on to that vision of himself. When he couldn't cope, he went back to alcohol. But every time he went back, he noticed he felt worse afterward. Instead of calming him down, drinking was making him feel more anxious and depressed.

Over time, Ben worked on releasing the anxiety and building his self-esteem (if you're looking for support in this area, go back to chapter 1). Without alcohol, he learned to face and cope with his emotions. He also learned to feel compassion for himself. Eventually, he accepted that his destructive behavior wasn't a statement about who he was; instead, it was rooted in his grief.

The more he understood how he was using alcohol to cope, the less he needed it to escape. He distanced himself from friends who wouldn't accept his sobriety. After multiple attempts, he finally got accepted into the fire department. Before long, he got a promotion, putting himself in line for a leadership position.

After years of sleeping with woman after woman, Ben fell in love with Robin, one of his fellow firefighters, a smart, driven, grounded woman who inspired him to commit. With her, he learned to trust that she and others wanted to know the real him, not the entertaining alpha male he was when he drank.

Though he fell down more than a few times along the way, Ben eventually changed his relationship with alcohol completely. It took years for him to work through his beliefs about himself and about what alcohol was doing for him, but he ultimately became the man he didn't think he could be.

By building his confidence and strengthening his connection with his true self, Ben eventually found his way to the career he wanted. This is the topic of our next chapter, where we'll focus on how you can find that career that's right for you, too.

PRACTICE

Pick a substance that's present in your life. Then ask yourself the following questions, and write down your answers:

How often do you use it?

Under what circumstances do you use it?

What are the drawbacks to using it?

What role did it play in your family? What did you learn from them about it?

What do you like about using it (i.e., what do you gain)?

Finally, ask yourself if there are benefits to using the substance that you'd like to create on your own. For example, would you like to feel socially confident without drinking alcohol? Or wake up naturally without needing caffeine? If the answer is 'yes,' then make a plan to take a break from that substance. Depending on how frequently you use it, you can either cut back or give it up entirely for a period of time.

As you experiment with cutting back or abstaining from that substance, write down what's happening for you. When is it difficult? When is it easy? What's surprising—or not surprising? What's interesting? What was the substance giving you—or taking away from you? Along the way, be sure to acknowledge yourself for taking steps to change your relationship with the substances in your life.

CHAPTER 7

HOW TO CREATE YOUR IDEAL CAREER

Since she was a child, my client Naomi wanted to work in fashion. She kept up with multiple fashion blogs and read piles of magazines. She followed fashion influencers on social media. As a teenager, she found jobs in clothing stores, determined to learn about every part of the industry. After she worked to support herself through college and design school, she landed a job at Neiman Marcus, where she dreamed of becoming a buyer.

After years of gradually working her way up, Naomi became head of the bridal suite at Neiman Marcus. She was more than thrilled. This was her dream job at her dream company. Initially, the work felt exciting and fulfilling.

However, as time went by, her initial feelings of excitement started to wear off: "I have a vision for fashion, but this isn't fulfilling," she told me. "And I don't think I really like customer service..." Besides being high-stress, the job made her feel empty.

Still, she wasn't ready to let it go. Wasn't this her path? After working so hard for so long, how could she walk away?

She couldn't imagine starting over. How could she possibly find a job that made her happy and fulfilled, had meaning, and paid well? If she did look for a new job, it had to fulfill all those criteria. Otherwise, it wasn't worth doing.

Or was it?

THE MYTH OF THE END-ALL, BE-ALL JOB

Unlike generations before them, millennials don't think of the highest-paying job as the ideal job. Instead, like Naomi, we're looking for careers that have meaning and purpose, jobs that encapsulate us and draw on our passions. We want to spend our professional lives participating in something that changes the world for the better and leaves a lasting impact.

Unfortunately, it's difficult to find careers that meet all our expectations. As a success coach as well as a therapist, I know that looking for the perfect job is the same thing as looking for a perfect mate—it doesn't exist.

Very few careers are going to check all your boxes. We often expect that we're going to walk into the office, change the world, and get paid the right amount of money for doing what we love. However, the truth is that it's extremely rare to find a job that meets all these expectations. As long as we're waiting for the perfect job, we run the risk of holding ourselves back from making a move that might help us grow.

Instead of waiting for the perfect job or the perfect company, the key to finding your ideal career is to look for work that helps you learn, grow, and draw on your strengths. Here are the steps you can take to get there.

STEP 1: GET CLEAR ON YOUR TRUE-SELF GOALS

One of the main reasons people don't achieve their career goals is that they can't see the difference between their true-self and negative-mind goals.

How can you tell the difference?

A negative mind goal is usually based on a desire for prestige, fame, and/or wealth. It ties your happiness to an external event or accomplishment. If you make a certain amount of money, if you get a job at company X, if you become a partner in a law firm by the time you're thirty, if you become a famous actor, then you'll feel happy and fulfilled.

The assumption behind negative mind goals is that somehow you're not enough. If, and only if, you achieve Y, you'll feel whole and complete. Instead of learning to create your own happiness, you base it on your next external accomplishment.

It may seem like a contradiction, but once you can get to a place where you feel whole and complete as you are, you open the way to finding and achieving your true-self goals. When you understand that your identity doesn't depend on your achievements, you free yourself to go after what you really want. In other words, detaching your sense of self-worth from your professional success helps you connect with the goals that are rooted in your true self. Instead of feeling desperate, like you *have to* achieve something, you feel inspired to go after it. And when you're feeling inspired, it's much easier to make good things happen in your life.

Sometimes it can be tricky to tell the difference between a true-self and a negative mind goal because the goal itself could fit into either category. For example, let's say you want to write a great book. If you're aiming to write the Great American Novel so everyone will know how talented and intelligent you are, it's a negative mind goal. On the other hand, if you want to write a book because you feel inspired to tell a particular story and you love the writing process itself, the goal is coming from your true self.

The difference between a true self and a negative mind goal isn't always black and white. The reality is that our goals contain elements of both, just like we as people contain elements of both. (As we discussed in chapter 4, sometimes we're fully in our negative mind or our true self, but most of the time, we're in both.) Our aim here is to ground our goals *primarily* in our true selves. This way, we continue to feel motivated to pursue them.

FIND YOUR STRENGTHS

If you're having trouble figuring out your true-self goals, start by taking an inventory of your strengths. Ask your family and friends what they think you're good at. Look back at positive experiences in your life and reflect on what you brought to them. Ask yourself if there are things that come easily to you that might be challenging for other people.

If you're not comfortable asking someone, or if you're looking for additional information about your strengths, try taking quizzes like StrengthsFinder or HIGH5 (high5test.com).

PICK A DIRECTION

Once you zero in on your strengths, the next step is to pick a direction. Do you want to be an artist? A software developer? A therapist? A firefighter? A game designer? When you're thinking about your career direction, try not to edit yourself. Though it might feel impossible when you start out, you want to take risks and pursue your big dreams, especially when you're in your twenties. This is the time in your life to go for it. The trick is to make a plan and take baby steps toward your big picture goals (which we'll explore in more detail in the sections below).

If you're already clear on your career direction but you're not sure where to start in terms of going after your dreams, feel free to skip ahead to the next section, where we explore how to uncover your blocks.

On the other hand, if you're still struggling to figure out what you're truly interested in, I'd like you to try out a strategy I use with many of my clients: approach your career the way you approach dating. Do you only go on dates with people who meet all your criteria? Most of us don't. We go out with people who seem attractive enough or smart enough. We try them on and see where it leads.

When you're looking for direction in your professional life, it helps to approach potential careers the way you'd approach a potential partner. Let's say you have ten strengths, and you find a job where you can apply three or four of them. Experiment and see where it leads. Does the work inspire you to go further on your chosen path? Does it open another door? Or does it make you want to change direction?

Though it may seem like a paradox, you often have to take a leap before you can clearly see where you want to go. Instead of sitting at home and worrying about which way to go, you're much more likely to find your direction if you're moving toward something.

In other words, the more action you take, the more opportunities you create. When you decide to enter the professional world, you not only build your skillset and resume, but you also meet people who can expose you to different ideas and possibilities—no matter which direction you choose.

STEP TWO: UNCOVER BLOCKS

Once you get clear about what you want and pick a direction, your negative mind will automatically kick in. Why? As we explored in chapters 3 and 4, the negative mind doesn't want anything in your life to change. Since it's rooted in your survival instinct, the negative mind wants your life to stay safe and predictable. It doesn't want you to take risks.

The fact is, though, that the moment you start taking baby steps toward your goals, you expose yourself to risk. So it's normal for limiting thought patterns to arise. Recognizing these thought patterns is the key to diminishing their power over you.

For my coaching clients, these are the five most common mental blocks that come up on the journey toward professional success:

1. **Undervaluing yourself:** The negative mind automatically focuses on your weaknesses and the reasons you're incapable of reaching your goals.

2. **Overestimating yourself:** Telling yourself that you don't want to start at the bottom, that you deserve more respect, or that you shouldn't have to work hard often cuts you off from making the most of your career opportunities.

3. **Taking things personally:** You think you're the cause of other people's negative behavior, which shakes your confidence and limits your perspective. When you interpret people's reactions as an attack on you or a reflection of their feelings toward you, you put yourself in a negative momentum loop. Ultimately, when you start to take things personally, you diminish your ability to give your best effort, whether it's at a networking event, an interview, or on the job.

4. **Thinking linearly instead of laterally:** You view the way to success as a linear path with an impossible number of steps between you and your goal—and you think you can predict how you're going to get there. The truth is, very few successful people describe their path as one that went from A to B to C to D. For example, my client Carlo started out at age seventeen working for minimum wage doing telemarketing for a loan company. Ultimately, he became a real estate investment broker

managing multi-million-dollar deals. When he was beginning his career, Carlo never imagined where his path would ultimately lead, but he committed to learning everything he could along the way, which opened doors he'd never anticipated.

5. **Having a "do-it-yourself" mentality:** You rely exclusively on yourself in going after your goals, giving the negative mind a greater sense of control. Too often, we underestimate the power of asking for (or offering) help and building relationships on our professional path. As we try to move up in the world, sometimes we forget that the connections we create are just as important—if not more important—than our talent.[12]

When I was working toward my goal of becoming a psychotherapist, I experienced almost all of these limiting thought patterns. The night before I started graduate school, I curled up on my bathroom floor and had a panic attack. My negative mind was practically shouting at me: "You're an awkward introvert who's good at math. What makes you think you can become a therapist?"

Eventually, I calmed myself down. I thought about why I wanted to become a therapist in the first place. I thought about my cousins, who had committed suicide in their twenties. I remembered the therapist who'd saved my life when I was a teenager.

---

12 If you're looking for more guidance on how to build relationships on your professional path, I recommend listening to this podcast with Adam Grant, the author of "Give and Take: Why Helping Others Drives Our Success": https://podtail.com/en/podcast/10-happier-with-dan-harris/-157-adam-grant-the-benefits-of-generosity/

Though I was terrified, I still showed up at school the next day. One of the first things we did was pair up and ask each other get-to-know-you questions. I was the youngest person in the program by a decade, and I thought I could see the condescension on my classmates' faces. But they were just mirroring my own insecurities.

When I went home that day, I felt exhausted and discouraged. How was I going to get from here to creating a private therapy practice? My goal felt impossibly far away.

So I took out a chair and tried this exercise.

THE EMPTY CHAIR: A FEAR-EASING EXERCISE

Bring two chairs into a room. Sit in one of them and speak from your negative mind. Express all your fears around your current goal, e.g., "I'm not good enough, smart enough, qualified enough."

Now switch chairs. Look at the empty chair where you spoke from your negative mind. One by one, address each of your fears: "Actually, I want to do this because there's a part of me that believes I can. And it would be so empowering to help young people change their lives."

Then switch back to the negative mind chair and offer a counterargument: "Yeah, but I'm so awkward. Who says I can get that confident part of myself in the room with my clients?"

Keep externalizing the dialog between your negative mind and your true self until your true self feels louder and more convincing than your negative mind.

BE PREPARED—AND BE PREPARED TO MAKE MISTAKES

As I was working toward becoming a therapist, another

technique I used to move past my limiting thought patterns was to prepare as much as possible for any given situation. In graduate school, I always did the required reading before every class—and more. This way, I was less afraid to speak up and ask questions. Even if I made a mistake, at least I knew I'd done my best.

I'd always been terrified of making mistakes. In grad school, I realized how much this fear had been holding me back. When we did in-class role-plays, I never volunteered to participate. I didn't want to humiliate myself in front of people who already seemed skeptical about me.

However, as I watched my classmates stumble through those role-plays, I realized that the point was actually to make mistakes. None of us knew what we were doing— which was why we were practicing. In fact, the role-plays actually worked better when one of us made a mistake because the professor would interject to teach us something new.

Eventually, I persuaded myself to volunteer for role-plays. Every time I did one, I reminded myself that my goal wasn't to be perfect. My goal was to grow.

ACKNOWLEDGE YOUR FEAR—AND TAKE ACTION

I volunteered for those role-plays even though I was afraid. If I'd waited until I released all my fears around making a mistake or humiliating myself, I never would have done it.

You're never going to overcome all your fears before you take action. It's natural to want to work through your fears before you take a step forward—but it's impossible to let go of everything you're afraid of. If you're waiting until all your fears disappear, you're holding yourself back.

You can acknowledge your fears and work through them to a certain extent. However, it's important to go a step further. The key here is to build up your confidence to the point where you're ready to act *while* you're feeling your fear.

Again, you don't have to erase all your fears before you do something. Whenever you're taking a risk—whether it's going to an interview, applying for an interesting-sounding job, or attending your first day of grad school—you don't have to feel 100 percent positive. Part of you may feel excited and inspired, while another part of you may feel terrified. This is natural.

The important thing is to go into that interview, apply for that job, or show up for class in spite of your fear. No matter what happens, when you take a step forward, you're being brave. You're giving yourself a chance to learn and make better decisions about your next move. You're also moving one step closer to the person you want to become in the professional world.

STEP THREE: MAKE A PLAN—AND TAKE BABY STEPS

When we set goals, our most common mistake is making the first step too big. While it's great to "think big," it's important to break down your goals into bite-sized pieces—or baby steps.

In other words, once you've picked a career direction (e.g., becoming an artist, a software developer, a firefighter, a voice actor) and have done the work to uncover your blocks, the next step is to work your way backward from your larger goal. What baby steps can you take right now, next month, and this year, to move toward this goal?

This is how I got through grad school and eventually became a therapist. In the beginning, I literally took things one day at a time: I focused on getting myself to class each day. Once that felt easy, I moved on to my next goal: volunteering for role-plays.

By starting small, I could easily track my progress. Not only that, as I continued to achieve my mini-goals, I built up my confidence and felt a sense of accomplishment.

So how do you create your baby step goals? The key is to make them specific, time-bound, clear, and manageable.

For example, a specific, time-bound, and manageable mini-goal would be applying to eight interesting jobs in the next month (versus finding a high-paying job you love). If you're working full-time and don't have time to apply to eight jobs, revisit your goal. Could you apply for one job per week? Or attend a networking[13] event once a month? The key is to pick things that are challenging but doable.

Don't worry about whether you're setting the "right" goals. The important thing is that your bite-sized goals inspire

---

13 If the idea of networking scares you, I recommend you check out "The Gift: A Revolution in Networking Mastery," by Matthew Ferry, et. al. When I was building my psychotherapy practice, this is the book that helped me get out there and build relationships via networking that help me to this day.

you to take action. Every time you take a baby step, you're coping with fear, building your self-esteem, and strengthening your relationship with your true self. As long as you feel these processes happening, it doesn't actually matter what you're doing. What matters is that you're doing it.

STEP FOUR: BE CONSISTENT

Having the discipline to apply consistent energy to your goals can be challenging, especially when you focus too much on the future.

As I was working toward becoming a psychotherapist, the thought of opening a private practice and actually seeing my first patient made me panic and want to give up. Over time, what helped me stay disciplined was reconnecting with my reasons for wanting to do the job in the first place.

What also helped me was learning to be in the moment. As I wrote in chapter 1, anxiety is always based on something we think might happen in the future. In graduate school, every time I imagined myself saying the wrong thing to a client, or not being able to help someone, or not having any clients at all, I realized my thoughts were based on my worst fears. They didn't correspond with my reality. If anything, they were pulling me away from my goal.

When you get sidetracked or feel tempted to give up on your goals, pause and ask yourself what's stopping you. It usually comes down to fear, but that fear can express itself in a variety of different ways. Sometimes it comes out as self-judgment (e.g., "I'm not good enough/smart enough."). Sometimes fear shows up in the form of fatigue or boredom, as when you suddenly feel exhausted when you start something challenging. Sometimes fear expresses itself as an urge to change direction and move on to the next best thing instead of working through your doubts and following through on your goals.

More often than not, we can trace our fears and negative coping mechanisms back to childhood. Why does this matter? Until we learn to recognize them, the same fears will continue to show up in different areas of our lives. For example, I went around for many years with the fear that I wasn't a person of value because I didn't think my parents wanted to be close to me. As I was working toward becoming a psychotherapist, my fear showed up in the form of self-judgment, which kept me from feeling confident about starting my own practice. In chapter 9, we'll go into more detail about how to break free from the fears and negative emotional patterns we develop in childhood.

In the meantime, the key is to identify your fear. Once you identify it, ask yourself what you need to come back to the present moment. If you've made a plan, go back to it and see how far you've come. Revisit your original inspirations. Remind yourself that every step you take, no matter how small it seems, is bringing you closer to your goal. And even if you think you've picked the wrong goal, being in action will still help you move more quickly toward the right one.

STEP 5: CELEBRATE

I've spent years building my psychotherapy practice, and I've celebrated every step of the way. After I saw my first client, I danced to my favorite song. When I signed my first five-year office lease, I booked a vacation.

I know a huge part of my success comes from learning how to be a master celebrator.

When you accomplish your goals, the negative mind automatically resists celebration: "This is ridiculous," your mind says. "All you did was X. But you really need to get to Y."

Your negative mind doesn't want you to feel complacent; it wants to feed into the idea that you're not good enough. While this idea might motivate you to move forward in the short term, it destroys your motivation over time. If your steps aren't big enough, or your actions not good enough, why keep going?

According to your negative mind, if you stop and celebrate, you won't be motivated to continue. However, the opposite is true: the act of celebrating creates a positive momentum loop. When you're in a positive momentum loop, you not only generate more hope for the future, you also feed your motivation, which makes it easier over time to take bigger and bolder steps toward your goals.

As adults, it can be challenging to build a positive momentum loop. Why? As children, we learned to be motivated by negative consequences. Generally, we were taught to get what we wanted by not creating trouble. As adults, we want to make a conscious switch to a positive momentum loop, where we learn to fire up our motivation by acknowledging our progress toward our goals—instead of mentally punishing ourselves when we fall short.

Besides helping you reach your goals, creating a positive momentum loop also empowers you to feel more fulfilled in the present. If you wait until you reach your "end" goal to reward yourself, you're missing out on all the times you could have made yourself happy in the process of getting there.

WHEN TO PIVOT

Let's imagine you've worked through all five of these steps. You're clear about your larger goals. You've identified your fears, made a plan, and consistently worked to achieve your goals. You've celebrated yourself every step of the way. But maybe you still don't feel like you're in the right place.

If you think it might be time to change direction, the first thing to do is give yourself full permission to pivot.

When Naomi, whose story opens this chapter, told me that her job as head of the bridal suite at Neiman Marcus's was unbearable, I reminded her that she was free. She didn't have to stay there. "This is the beauty of being a human being, at least in the United States," I said to her. "You can do whatever you want."

I asked Naomi to take a day[14] and live in that place of feeling free. "Tell yourself you're going to quit," I said, "Imagine it's going to end." Then I asked her to write down all the feelings that came up. Did it feel freeing? Sad? Was she

---

14 Some decisions are more time-sensitive than others. If a decision feels urgent but isn't time sensitive, take more time—several days, a week, a month—to live as if you've decided one way or the other. The bigger the decision you need to make, the more time you need to keep coming back to it.

relieved? What was she missing? What were the positives and negatives?

The next day, Naomi did the same exercise, only this time, she told herself she would stay in her current job. Then she wrote down all the emotions that scenario brought up for her. In this situation, it was important for Naomi to fully live in one scenario without the interference of the other. If she kept bouncing back and forth between the two scenarios, she was in danger, feeding her feelings of anxiety—and getting stuck.

Living as if she'd decided one way, then switching to living the other way for the same period of time helped Naomi find clarity. Putting herself in both situations and noting how she felt helped lower the volume of her negative mind. By setting aside her thoughts about how long and hard she'd worked to get where she was, she created space to connect with the goals and desires from her true self.

Still, Naomi went back and forth on her decision for over a month. Besides needing time to lower the volume on the voice in her negative mind, she was also caught up in other people's opinions. Would her parents think she was a flake? Would her boss get angry? When she finally shut out those voices, the feeling of gnawing anxiety went away. She caught herself smiling when she thought about quitting. The pain in her shoulders started to fade.

She knew she was ready to quit her job, but she was afraid to change direction. Instead of looking for the perfect new career, I suggested she start by asking the people in her life if they knew of any interesting jobs.

A few weeks later, one of her co-workers at Neiman Marcus told her about a job managing the company's new packing facility. A packing facility? Naomi was skeptical at first. It didn't sound fun or glamorous at all. But she'd grown so miserable as the head of the bridal suite that she decided to give it a try.

Before long, Naomi fell in love with her new job. For one thing, she was relieved to be away from customer service. On top of that, she was figuring out ways to make the warehouse system work, which turned out to be a perfect fit for her organizational skills.

Even though she was younger than the people she was managing, she felt how much they appreciated having a responsible boss who listened to them, created a clear structure, and made things run smoothly.

BE IN IT FULLY AND FIND THE MEANING

Over time, Naomi continued to set herself up for success. Not only because she was willing to try out an unlikely job, but also because she was able to be in her work fully and find the meaning in what she was doing.

When Naomi started her new job, the advice I gave her was the advice I give all my clients: Find the meaning in whatever you're doing. Don't do anything passively. Don't think of your actions as a means to an end. Be in them fully.

"The key to becoming successful," I told her, "is to go into work every day giving 110 percent. Don't obsess about what everyone else is contributing. Don't think about what might be above your pay grade. Anticipate what people need instead of waiting for them to ask you. And treat the company as if you own part of it."

Naomi wasn't just managing a packing facility. She was making a difference in people's work lives and, by extension, their home lives. Creating a positive environment in the warehouse, where she and her co-workers spent most of their time, gave her a deep, lasting sense of fulfillment. Besides that, by making her boss and colleagues feel good about themselves and their work, she was also building connections that will eventually help her when she's ready to make her next career move.

By giving all of herself to her work, Naomi was supporting her growth; she was also continuing to open herself to paths that might not be immediately visible. As she learned to find the meaning in what she was doing, she connected with her true self, uncovered her strengths, and developed a clearer picture of her potential.

In the meantime, she also cleared the way toward reaching her financial goals, which is the subject of our next chapter.

PRACTICE

Make a list of your career goals. Now take time to look at each item on the list and notice the emotions that come up around each goal.

Choose the three goals that feel the most exciting to you and circle those.

What steps do you need to take in order to reach these goals? Break down these steps into smaller and smaller steps until you can see the first baby step. This is the one that feels challenging yet doable right now.

Now create a monthly plan and map out the baby steps you're going to take during that month.

After you finish writing out your monthly plan, think about the blocks that might come up for you as you try to execute it, e.g., undervaluing yourself, taking things personally, thinking linearly, trying to do everything on your own.

Journal about how you're going to address each block as it comes up. For example, if you tend to undervalue yourself, commit to going back to noting your strengths. If you often take things personally, remind yourself that people are more worried about themselves than they are about you; you can't know the meaning behind their behavior. If you lean toward thinking linearly, keep coming back to the moment (e.g., "I can't predict the future, so I'm just going to follow my plan step-by-step."). If you tend to do everything on your own, look for people you can ask for help or collaborate with; seek out people to whom you have something to offer, and who can offer you something as well.

After you reflect on potential blocks, think about how you're going to cel-ebrate every time you take a baby step—and write it down. Along the way, you'll reach certain milestones that deserve bigger celebrations, like signing up for a class you've been wanting to take, taking yourself out for dinner and a movie, or having a spa day at home. Think about what these celebrations will be and write those down, too.

If you get sidetracked, try not to get angry at yourself. Instead, remember that being on a growth path means falling off the wagon sometimes: the key isn't always staying on the wagon—it's getting back on as quickly as possible when you fall off. This way, you keep building your positive momentum loop, which will empower you to take bigger and bigger steps toward your goals over time.

CHAPTER 8

HOW TO HAVE A HEALTHY RELATIONSHIP WITH MONEY

My client Craig grew up in a lower-middle-class family, the only child of a single mom. Though they never had much money, Craig's mom wanted to give him everything he wanted. After spending most of her money on him, his mom would struggle to pay the rent at the end of the month.

Meanwhile, Craig dreamed of becoming a television writer. Eventually, he got a scholarship to USC, where he struggled to fit in. He felt like his classmates were a bunch of spoiled rich kids who didn't have a care in the world.

"Rich people are empty," he thought. Empty was the last thing he wanted to be.

After he graduated from USC, Craig slowly worked his

way up in the entertainment world. Though he felt like he was progressing toward becoming a TV writer, he also felt something holding him back whenever he took a step closer to his goal.

"Basically," he said, "I'm afraid I can't have money and be a good person."

YOUR RELATIONSHIP WITH MONEY

Craig thought of money as an unimportant part of his life that had nothing to do with his emotions. He didn't want to focus on it or devote any energy into it. However, by avoiding his relationship with money, he was preventing himself from getting what he wanted.

Though you may not necessarily think of it as a separate relationship, your relationship with money is actually an emotional process, just like your relationships with your family, your friends, and your romantic partners. Your beliefs about money and the role it plays in your life not only affect how you live, but they also impact the way you relate to other people.

What shapes your beliefs about money? And how do you change those beliefs? The first step is to look at the role money played in your family.

INSPECT YOUR FINANCIAL UPBRINGING

How much money did your family have? How did they relate to that money? The answers to these questions are the key to helping you understand your current relationship with money.

Did you grow up poor? Middle class? Wealthy? Somewhere in between? If your family was poor, was there a feeling of anxiousness about not having enough or was your family content with what they had?

If you grew up wealthy, did you feel like your family was always striving for more? Or was there a sense of gratitude around the abundance? How much did your family understand that money didn't define them?

For Craig, and for many of my clients, there was always a feeling of anxiousness around money in the family. Growing up without it led him to distrust people who had it.

Though he didn't want to feel anxious about money, or handle it poorly like his mom did, he was afraid that having money would end up defining him. He didn't want money to become his identity. So he avoided thinking about it altogether.

MYTHS AND STEREOTYPES

Besides your upbringing, the many myths and stereotypes around money in our culture also shape your relationship with it. Understanding how these myths might influence your beliefs around money is another key to developing a healthy relationship with it.

MYTH #1: MAKING MONEY EQUALS HAPPINESS

Money isn't the root of happiness. We understand this idea intellectually, but it's more challenging to internalize it emotionally. Like my client Lilly, many of us are waiting to be happy until we have a certain amount of money.

Lilly grew up poor, on a farm in the middle of a small town in Ecuador in a family where scarcity created a high level of emotional stress. When she decided to come to the United States, she vowed to leave her past behind. She wanted to create a new life. She promised herself she'd never be poor again.

Lilly learned English as quickly as she could (her first language was Spanish). She went to networking events. She applied for hundreds of jobs. Eventually, she found work in sales.

Before long, she was making over six figures. But it still wasn't enough. The people in her life, including potential romantic partners, could sense her desperation around money. It became a barrier to emotional intimacy.

Lilly had gone beyond her financial goals, so why didn't she feel happy?

Once you reach a certain point financially, income stops correlating with happiness. According to a Princeton University study that examined the connection between emotional well-being and income, respondents' assessments of their lives rose along with their incomes. However, once they were making approximately $75,000 per year, their everyday emotional experiences stopped improving. In other words, after you meet your basic needs, and have enough money to do the things that make you feel fulfilled, the amount of money you make actually doesn't matter much.[15]

---

15   Daniel Kahneman and Angus Deaton, "High Income Improves Evaluation of Life But Not Emotional Well Being," *PNAS* 107, no. 38 (2010): 16489-16493.

MYTH #2: SPENDING MONEY EQUALS HAPPINESS

Besides equating making money with happiness, sometimes we think spending money will fill some sort of emotional void. When my client Keri starts feeling down, for example, she likes to buy things to make herself feel better.

In the short-term, going shopping makes her happy. If she buys clothes, say, she gets excited about presenting an updated, more attractive version of herself to the world.

But the happiness doesn't last. Besides that, after the money runs out, she realizes she's further away from reaching her long-term financial goals, like moving out of her parents' house and taking a trip around the world. In the end, spending money to distract herself from the emotions she needs to process doesn't make her feel any better. After the shine wears off what she buys, her negative feelings are still there—and her financial situation feels more unmanageable.

MYTH #3: HAVING MONEY EQUALS HAVING PERSONAL VALUE

One of the most powerful messages in our wealth-driven culture is that money makes us more valuable as human beings. My client Mike, a first-generation American who grew up in a lower-middle-class family, was a perfect example of this way of thinking: "If I have a million dollars in the bank," he thought, "then I'll really feel like I achieved something great."

So he got to work, teaching himself everything there was to know about the savings and loan industry. By the time he was twenty-three, he'd reached his goal. He had a million dollars in the bank.

But looking at his bank statement only made him feel empty. As he struggled with that emptiness, he became addicted to drugs. Eventually, he lost all the money.

Mike assumed that becoming a millionaire would make him feel important. Once he had the money, he expected his insecurities and his uncertainty about his identity to vanish. In the end, when he realized the money didn't define him, or make him more valuable as a person, he felt lost.

MYTH #4: HAVING MONEY LEADS TO GREED AND SHALLOWNESS

"I don't want to be one of *those* people." I hear this idea from a lot of clients, including Craig, whose story opens this chapter. In his mind, being wealthy meant being greedy and shallow.

Having money doesn't make you empty, though. And being wealthy doesn't mean you're greedy or shallow (or better than anyone else). It's how you earn money, and what you do with it, that impacts you as a person.

When you have money, you have the power to create your own experience with it. You can choose to hoard it and be greedy. You can create new possibilities for yourself with it. You can use it to help others. Money doesn't automatically make you a good or bad person. What counts is what you do with it.

ASSESSING YOUR RELATIONSHIP WITH MONEY

Your upbringing and experience, plus cultural myths and stereotypes, are the main influences on your relationship with your finances. Before we explore ways to create a healthy relationship with money, it's important to be aware of your starting point. Where are you right now in your relationship with money?

Most of us can categorize our relationship with money in terms of three main styles of attachment: anxious, avoidant, and secure. (We'll explore the idea of attachment styles in more detail in chapter 9.)

If you're **anxious** about money, all of your decisions around money involve saving it or finding ways to make more of it. Money brings up feelings of desperation.

In an **avoidant** relationship with money, you push your finances aside and refuse to deal with things like creating a budget, saving, or setting goals.

A **secure** relationship with money is just what it sounds like: you believe it's available when you need it, and you're open to seeing what it can do for you. Being generous with money feels natural and fun.

Your relationship with money might be a combination of two or even all three of the attachment styles. The important thing to think about is which one(s) best describe your relationship with money at this point in your life.

Another thing to keep in mind is that we're all on a continuum when it comes to these attachment styles. Imagine anxious is on one end of the continuum, avoidant is on the other, and secure is in the middle. Depending on how we're triggered, we move back and forth on the continuum; how much we move varies based on our starting point as well as the person and the situation that's triggering us.

Wherever you happen to be on the continuum, your attachment to money is something you're capable of transforming.

HOW TO CREATE A HEALTHY RELATIONSHIP WITH MONEY

You can create a healthy relationship with money. It only takes four steps, which we'll walk through together, going back to Craig's story as an example.

STEP 1: RECOGNIZE YOUR BELIEFS

With Craig, the aspiring TV writer, the process of changing his relationship with money started with recognizing the nature of his attachment to it.

Telling himself money wasn't important, refusing to focus on his finances, and categorizing rich people as empty were aspects of his avoidant relationship with money. These were beliefs he used to mask his fear around money.

As long as he was living in the thought that he couldn't have money and be happy, that money was empty, and that it would turn him into a shallow person, Craig couldn't change his relationship with money. Only when he acknowledged his beliefs could he start to transform them.

STEP 2: FIND YOUR FEAR

When he became conscious of his beliefs around money, Craig cleared the way to look for the fear underneath them. This is the second step in changing your relationship with money: identifying the emotion that's driving the talk in your head.

In Craig's case, there were two main fears: "Actually, I'm really scared, Jesse, that I'm not going to be able to make money. And even if I do, I won't know how to manage it. I feel like I won't ever have enough money to do the things I want to do."

This was Craig's root vulnerability. Once he found it, he expressed it. He allowed himself to feel it. Then he started to address it.

STEP 3: DECIDE WHAT YOU WANT

After he got clear about his root fears around money, Craig asked himself how he wanted to relate to it. What did he like about the way his family handled money? What would he change? What did he want? Why did he want it?

Connect to a Money Goal

The first thing Craig did was set a money goal. However, his goal had to go beyond a number. It had to come from his true self.

What did he want to *do* with that money? What would be exciting to him? Owning a house? Booking a trip to Costa

Rica? Signing up for yoga classes at his favorite studio? Being able to take his friends to dinner?

Once he connected to the material things and/or experiences that were exciting for him, the next step was to identify the feelings he associated with reaching his money goals. Would having or doing certain things make him feel empowered? Secure? Successful? Or was his money goal more about filling a void or living up to other people's expectations?

When you're thinking about your money goals, the trick is to feel inspired about them at your core. At the same time, you don't want to choose a money goal that makes you feel like less of a person because you haven't reached it yet.

Along those lines, it's important to avoid postponing your happiness while you're trying to reach your money goals. Look at most successful entrepreneurs: it's the *process* of going after their vision that brings them happiness and fulfillment. On their way to financial success, the founders of companies like Whole Foods, Spanks, and Wikipedia enjoyed the steps they took to make big things happen as much as (if not more than) the end results of their hard work.[16]

Ultimately, as I told Craig, you want to tie your money goals to things that fulfill you in your soul. When you make that connection, you fire up your motivation to stay focused on your financial aspirations, even when things get challenging.

---

16   To learn more about the stories behind these entrepreneurs' success, listen to the podcast *How I Built This with Guy Raz* on NPR: https://www.npr.org/podcasts/510313/how-i-built-this.

STEP 4: MAKE A PLAN

Besides being intimidated by the idea of a budget, Craig resisted creating one because he thought it would be stifling.

When I asked him things like how much money he was bringing in, what his expenses were, and whether he had enough money to meet them, he wanted to run in the other direction.

What I eventually helped him understand was that having a clear picture of his income and expenses would allow him to think about what he wanted in his life. How much more would he need to make to add activities that felt exciting and fulfilling?

Once he saw his budget on paper, it felt much less intimidating to him. It also gave him the confidence to move out of his mother's house.

Still, living on his own was a challenge at first. Going from spending whatever he wanted to paying rent and limiting himself to basic expenses was a big shift. He bought things he didn't need. He felt frustrated about not having enough money to travel or go out with his friends. He had trouble figuring out the difference between his wants and his needs—because he'd never had to think about them before.

"Why am I doing this?" he asked me. "I could be living rent-free at home and shopping at Whole Foods. Why am I putting all this pressure on myself to suffer?"

"Because managing your own finances makes you more likely to succeed," I told him. I shared with him the experiences of other young people I knew: the ones who became financially independent from their parents/caregivers, either by choice or necessity, were more successful and more fulfilled than the ones who depended on their parents/caregivers for financial support.

Think about it: it's a huge confidence boost to go out into the world and discover that you're able to survive on your own. Even if you're doing a job that doesn't feel glamorous, you're proving to yourself that you can create your own future.

Over time, Craig settled into his budget. He learned to see what was important and what he could do without. Eventually, he mapped out how he wanted to set himself up for the future. As he took more and more control of his finances, his fear around money changed to excitement.

BRING IN FINANCIAL ROLE MODELS

As Craig became more confident about his finances, he also worked his way up in the entertainment world. To jump-start his career, he started inviting people in the industry to lunch.

Besides helping him make connections with people in his field, those lunch meetings also introduced him to people who were successful and wealthy—*and* generous, selfless, and fulfilled. Meeting people who'd worked their way to the top on their own, professionally and financially, was inspiring to him. In them, he found proof that it was possible to have money and be a good person.

When you're working to redefine your relationship with

money, it's important to surround yourself with people who are more successful than you are—and who relate to money the way you want to.

You probably know the old saying, "The people you surround yourself with are who you become." If you associate with people who embody what you want to accomplish, you begin to see that it's possible for you, too. You also learn how to lay the foundation for your financial future.[17]

Eventually, Craig worked his way into a writer's room at a popular sit-com. Besides setting himself up in a nice apartment, going to exercise classes, and traveling, he's working toward being able to help his mom financially—and treat her to things she couldn't afford on her own.

Once he faced his fears around money, Craig stopped holding himself back from achieving what he wanted. In the process of changing his relationship with money, he not only reached his financial and professional goals, he also learned to treat money the way he treated the other relationships in his life. He couldn't be careless with it. He had to invest time in it and make sacrifices for it. He had to figure out what was in his control—and learn to let go of what wasn't.

In Part III, we're going to move from your relationship with money to the other relationships in your life, begin-

---

17 Wealthy people don't just work and save their money; they invest, and they know how to be strategic with their money. For example, they buy houses instead of renting. But they don't just buy any house: they do their research, investigating whether the house they buy is likely to increase in value over time. As you look for financial role models, it's important to connect with people who know how to make smart choices with their money—and ask them for guidance.

ning with the very first relationships you ever have: your parents/caregivers.

PRACTICE

Take a few minutes to write about your family's relationship with money. Were they secure around money? Anxious or angry because they didn't have enough? Grateful for the money they had? What did they think their income level said about them?

Now take a few minutes to write about your own relationship with money. What, if any, are your fears around money? What did you adopt from your family's relationship with money? What did you rebel against?

In the context of your relationship with money, write down your money goals. Include your money goals for the month, the quarter, and the year.

Then create a budget to help you reach those money goals. What is your income? What are your expenses? Are you able to meet your basic needs? If so, what do you need to do in order to reach your financial goals? If not, how much do you need in order to meet your basic needs—and what can you do to get there? (Hint: If you need help creating a budget and tracking your spending, experiment with free apps like Mint or PocketGuard.)

In the meantime, seek out financial role models. Is there someone in your life whose relationship with money you admire, or who's further along than you when it comes to finances? Invite them out for a beverage and ask them about their path to financial success. How did they get there? What did they learn along the way? What would they change if they did it all over again?

PART III

RELATIONSHIPS

CHAPTER 9

HOW TO REALIGN YOUR RELATIONSHIP WITH YOUR PARENTS— AND YOURSELF

My client Karine grew up with parents who both were physically and emotionally abusive. Though her father wasn't around much, things always turned dramatic when he showed up. But Karine was and is a fiery soul. Instead of submission, her response was to fight back.

By the time she turned fifteen, living at home felt unbearable. Karine and her parents constantly fought, and more often than not, the situation escalated into violence. Finally Karine's aunt decided it was too dangerous for Karine to stay with her parents. Karine moved in with her aunt.

After she moved out of her parents' house, Karine's life stabilized. Over time, her focus shifted from drinking, partying, and getting into fights to studying, getting sober, working out, and picking better friends. She graduated high school and went on to junior college. She'd always been good with numbers, so she decided to study accounting.

In her teens, Karine went from one boyfriend to the next, dating a string of men who abused and cheated on her. In her twenties she met Henry. Right away, she could feel that he was different from others she'd dated.

Henry had grown up in an abusive household, too. He'd coped by taking care of his mom and constantly trying to keep the peace. In his relationship with Karine, he did everything he could to make her feel good.

At first, they had a beautiful connection. They understood one another. They had fun. They even made up their own language. But as time went by, their relationship turned explosive. Every week, they went from one extreme to the other, arguing to the point of breaking up, then making up afterward.

"It's him," Karine said. "He won't get a job. He never cleans up after himself." She spent entire sessions picking Henry apart. However, there was more to the story than what he was doing wrong.

Karine didn't realize she was recreating the experience she'd had with her parents. She didn't know she was unconsciously replaying the emotional soundtrack that she'd grown up with. How could she know? Until then, it was the only soundtrack she'd listened to.

WHY WE NEED TO EXAMINE OUR RELATIONSHIP WITH OUR PARENTS/CAREGIVERS

The relationship you have with your parents or your primary caregivers is the blueprint for all of your intimate emotional relationships. No matter how that relationship played out during your childhood, your experience with your parents/caregivers is something you bring into relationships throughout your life, especially your romantic ones.

During your childhood, you learn to establish patterns of relating with your parents or your primary caregivers. Once you reach adulthood, it's natural to take these established patterns from childhood and apply them to all of your relationships.

However, as Karine's story shows us, if you unconsciously carry negative patterns from your childhood in your adult relationships, it's destined to lead to problems. If you ignore what happened in your past, it inhibits your ability to create the kind of emotional intimacy you want in the present.

So how do you break free from your old patterns? The first step is to become aware of how you learned to cope with the level of emotional intimacy you experienced as a child.

HOW DID YOU LEARN TO COPE AS A CHILD?

If you think of your childhood as a movie, it's helpful to imagine the emotional character of your family as the soundtrack. That soundtrack—whether it was violent and dramatic, cold and reserved, warm and inviting, or uneven and intense—was your experience of the world.

Just like a movie soundtrack, the emotional soundtrack in your family fluctuates. It's made up of many different notes. As much as it varies, however, your family's emotional soundtrack still creates a unique atmosphere and an overall tone.

At some point during your childhood, you establish behavioral patterns to fit the emotional soundtrack in your family. As you get older, you unconsciously re-create your family's emotional soundtrack in your adult relationships. If you grew up in an explosive environment like Karine, for example, you might fall into a pattern of starting dramatic arguments with your friends or your partner. On the other hand, if your parents/caregivers avoided talking about their feelings, re-creating your family's emotional soundtrack could mean sidestepping your true feelings and trying to keep things "polite."

The emotional soundtrack you grew up with also set the stage for the level of emotional intimacy you experienced in your family. In any family, intimacy naturally fluctuates between closeness and distance. However, every family has an overall average level of intimacy—and that level of intimacy is what you carry into your adult relationships, especially your romantic ones.

In other words, the emotional soundtrack you grew up with, along with the corresponding level of emotional intimacy in your family, become your reference points for relationships and emotional closeness in adulthood. The more awareness you have around these emotional patterns from childhood, the easier it is to choose what you want to keep—and what you're ready to let go of.

BLAMING YOUR PARENTS/CAREGIVERS VERSUS BLAMING YOURSELF

While you were growing up, if you lacked emotional intimacy, or if you found yourself in an upsetting scenario at home, there were two ways to look at the situation: it was either your fault or your parents'/caregivers' fault.

Why did you see the world this way? As children, we're developmentally self-centered. Since we're not yet capable of abstract thought, we can only see things in black and white.

1. Parent's/Caregiver's Fault	2. Your Fault
BENEFIT: Your self-worth stays intact.	**BENEFIT:** The people taking care of you always know what is best for you. If they're not giving you the emotional support you need, or if something goes wrong, you only have to figure out how to make it right.
DRAWBACK: The people in charge of meeting your needs are not perfect. Therefore the world can be a scary and unpredictable place.	**DRAWBACK:** Your self-worth diminishes because you/your actions are responsible if anything upsetting happens.

There's no way our parents/caregivers can meet all our emotional needs as children—they're only human. However, for most of us, this idea is too frightening, and too difficult to understand, in childhood.

Unless you had highly dysfunctional caregivers, you probably erred on the side of blaming yourself if you didn't get your emotional needs met. Why? Because it's safer. The idea that your parents/caregivers aren't perfect is a terrifying thing to believe as a kid. After all, these are the people you're depending on for survival. If they don't know how to take care of you, then who's going to meet your needs?

As a child, you think everything revolves around you, so you grow up believing everything is your creation. You think that by doing certain things, or behaving a certain way, you'll get what you need. In other words, you want to believe you're in control of your survival. By taking on that responsibility, you feel less afraid.

Ultimately, though, when you make the decision to blame yourself for the fact that your caregivers couldn't meet all your emotional needs, you develop beliefs about yourself that aren't true. If you're not conscious of these beliefs, you take them into your adult relationships. Like Karine, whose story opens this chapter, you continue to recreate the soundtrack and emotional intimacy level of your childhood—even when you want to rewrite them.

COMMON FALSE BELIEFS AND NEGATIVE COPING MECHANISMS

We all have imperfect parents/caregivers. However, as I mentioned above, most of us don't want to believe our caregivers are imperfect. As a child, it's easier to take on the belief that *we're* imperfect. Growing up, we make up certain stories and false beliefs to support this idea. Then we develop negative coping mechanisms to back up our false beliefs.

How do you recognize these false beliefs? They usually fall into two categories, though you tend to fluctuate between the two depending on the circumstances: Either you convince yourself that you're inferior to everyone else (not loveable, not good enough) or you develop the belief that you're superior.

For example, I grew up in a home where the emotional soundtrack could be distant at times; at certain moments it wasn't easy for my parents to deal with my sensitivities, vulnerabilities, and fears. Since I couldn't wrap my childhood brain around the idea that my parents weren't always capable of meeting my emotional needs, I developed the belief that I was unlovable. In order to cope with that belief, I decided to make myself loveable.

I learned how to anticipate everyone else's needs, how to take care of people, how to make them feel important—and make them love me in return. However, in seeking everyone else's love, I didn't learn how to love myself. As I got older, I looked for the love and security I didn't experience in childhood in all of my relationships.

Meanwhile, my client Damien developed the belief that he was better than everyone else. The first time he came to me for therapy, he complained that he couldn't connect with other people because he was "light years ahead of them." There was some truth in what he was saying. There were moments during our conversation when he seemed more like a fifty-year-old professor than the scruffy, slightly overweight eighteen-year-old he was.

The longer we worked together, the more I saw that his

superiority was just a mask. Like a lot of my male clients, Damien grew up feeling like a disappointment to his parents, so he developed the belief that he wasn't smart enough. His arrogance was a way to cope with that belief.

All of us have different ways of coping with the false beliefs we develop as children. Some of us get angry, cut ourselves, and/or fall into addiction. Some of us learn to isolate ourselves emotionally or give so much to others we forget to love ourselves.

As you transition into adulthood, you can learn to recognize the false beliefs and negative coping mechanisms you adopted as a child—and forgive yourself for the way you dealt with them.

FORGIVE YOURSELF FOR HOW YOU COPED

Before we explore how to rewrite your false beliefs and re-work your negative coping mechanisms, I want to make one thing clear: your beliefs and the negative coping mechanisms you developed around them were what helped you survive. They were the best way to deal with your situation at the time, so it's important not to judge yourself for the way you coped.

After my cousin committed suicide, I fluctuated between being unable to cry and feeling completely overwhelmed by grief. I had no place to put my pain. My body started to disassociate, and I went numb. So I started to cut myself. Most people, including my first therapist, classified my behavior as crazy.

Then I met Toni, the therapist who changed my life. Instead of judging me for the way I was coping with my pain, she actually gave me credit for it: "That was smart, Jesse," she said. "You figured out how to deal with your pain. And you found a way to soothe yourself. If you hadn't figured that out, you wouldn't have made it."

Toni recognized that I didn't have other coping skills at that time in my life to deal with my pain. Until that point, cutting was my solution. It helped me stay sane and remain in my body.

Once you uncover your old patterns and decide you want to change them, it's important to start the process by forgiving yourself for developing those patterns in the first place. As a kid, you did whatever you had to do to get your needs met.

However, those coping mechanisms might not be serving you any longer.

ATTACHMENT STYLES

Once you're aware of the beliefs and negative coping mechanisms you developed during childhood, the next step is to look at how those beliefs are affecting your ability to form attachments, or your attachment style.

Learning about the different attachment styles—and looking at which one(s) reflect your experience—is an important part of rewriting old patterns that might have a negative impact on your current relationships.

As I mentioned in chapter 8, attachment styles fall into

three main categories: secure, anxious, and avoidant. However, there are also subcategories within these primary attachment styles. With the exception of the secure attachment style, each one represents what you learned to do in response to your unmet dependency needs.

Before we look at the characteristics of the different attachment styles, I want to make two things clear. First, attachment styles are not a diagnosis. Once you identify your attachment style(s) and see how it's affecting your relationships, you also have the ability to transform it. In other words, it's not a psychological sentence.

The other thing I want to emphasize in relation to attachment styles is that there are *styles* and *states*. Attachment *styles* are relatively fixed—but again, you're capable of transforming them. Attachment *states* are constantly fluctuating. Certain people or situations can trigger you, causing your state to change.

For example, disagreements can trigger different states of attachment. If you're thinking the other person is wrong, you're in an avoidant state. If you're thinking you're in the wrong, you're in an anxious state. If you're in a secure state, no one is wrong; you just have different perspectives.

WHAT'S YOUR ATTACHMENT STYLE?

Let's examine the basic characteristics of each attachment style and its subcategories to see which one best describes you, keeping in mind that you can flip between categories depending on your circumstances.

ANXIOUS

Fear of uncertainty is the core experience of this attachment style. It's difficult to let go when you're separating, and it's difficult to be soothed when you're reuniting. No amount of affection feels like enough. You feel calm when you're close to someone. Others sometimes feel suffocated by you.

Subcategory: Anxious Avoidant

If you're anxious avoidant, you live in an ambivalent state. You're afraid to be too close or too distant from others. You flip back and forth between independence and dependence. You get angry when others don't help you, but you also tend to feel suffocated when someone is trying to meet your emotional needs. The people you want to be with are the same people you're frightened to be close to.

AVOIDANT

The avoidant attachment style is characterized by detachment. Though you can be charismatic and fun, you don't let people know what you actually need. You may take care of others, but it's hard for you to lean on them in any way. Your partners often feel like a relationship with you is one-sided.

Subcategory: Dismissive Avoidant

As a dismissive avoidant type, you sacrifice your internal life in order to function. You completely detach from what you need in order to take care of what everyone else needs, so you can't feel anything, even in a positive sense. You don't feel any distress at separation or joy at reunion. You minimize the importance of relationships.

SECURE

If you're secure in your attachments, you're capable of giving and receiving love. You don't have to sacrifice your needs for someone else; you're confident you can both get your needs met. Disagreements don't scare you; you know relationships can survive them. You're flexible in how you relate to people and you understand their perspective.

> If you're unsure about which style best describes you, take this attachment style quiz: testyourself.psychtests.com/testid/2859. Keep in mind that the results of this quiz describe your dominant attachment style. However, your attachment style can change over time and in different situations.

HOW TO TRANSFORM YOUR ATTACHMENT STYLE

Once you recognize your attachment style, you have the ability to change it. At the same time, it's important to proceed without judgment. Remember: your attachment style is a response to emotional needs that weren't met during your childhood. Try to hold on to this idea as you work toward healing your attachment injuries.

FROM ANXIOUS TO SECURE

How do you move from an anxious or avoidant to a secure attachment style? Let's start with an example of someone with an anxious attachment style.

My client Maya spent her early dating life revolving around her romantic partners and trying to anticipate their needs. Her relationship with Jake was no exception; she did everything she could to make him happy, from cooking dinner to buying him special treats to sending him affectionate texts every day. Her logic was: "If he's happy, I'm happy."

Over time, though, Jake could feel that his happiness wasn't Maya's true motivation. Though she thought she was being an incredible girlfriend, she was actually making him responsible for her well-being. The truth was she couldn't feel calm, centered, or happy unless she had Jake's attention.

As is almost always the case, there was history behind her behavior: Maya grew up in a home with a verbally abusive mother and an emotionally absent father. Since she couldn't attach to either of her parents, she developed low self-esteem and became desperate for connection. Not being conscious of them, she brought these negative emotional patterns into her relationship with Jake.

As time went by, Jake's feelings for Maya started to fade. He no longer felt the excitement he experienced when they first met. He wasn't sure he wanted to stay in the relationship. However, the more he distanced himself, the more Maya chased him. Pretty soon, Jake felt so suffocated he was on the verge of breaking up with her. When she felt him pulling away, Maya started to have panic attacks. That's when she sought me out for help.

When she first came to see me, Maya felt like her entire life depended on her relationship with Jake. She was focusing every fiber of her being on not losing him. Though it was extremely difficult for her, Maya gradually learned to refocus her attention on herself instead of on Jake. We worked in baby steps. In the beginning, instead of reaching out to Jake for reassurance, she reached out to me or other people in her life.

Ultimately, what helped Maya move away from her anxious attachment style was re-connecting with herself and her own goals and passions. Little by little, she shifted her energy to her career. As an extrovert, she loved talking with people and had great social skills; she translated those skills into being a community manager for a growing start-up.

As Maya grew more successful, her confidence skyrocketed. She stopped tying her self-esteem to the way Jake felt about her. She realized she could survive without him. "I still love him and want to be with him," she said. "But if it's not right, I have my career, and I'm going to be fine."

The more secure she felt, the more attractive she became. Before long, Jake was the one chasing after her.

FROM AVOIDANT TO SECURE

Though he was a sensitive person who felt things deeply, Tony grew up in a family where no one knew how to process their feelings. When he was eight, his parents divorced, and his father moved away. The atmosphere at home wasn't abusive. However, there was no room for Tony to feel upset about the divorce—or about anything else.

When he was twenty-two, Tony came to me for therapy. He felt like he was walking through life in a haze; he couldn't feel anything. As a child, he'd learned that his feelings were too much, so he adopted an avoidant attachment style.

By developing an addiction to Internet porn, Tony did what many avoidant types do: he engaged in behaviors that are attachment-related but don't actually involve attachment.

"There's a moment after I masturbate and look at porn when I feel euphoric and alive," he said. However, the feeling would last just seconds before he fell into a self-hating spiral, getting angry with himself for giving in to his addiction.

What helped Tony gradually move away from an avoidant attachment style was being aware of where it came from. Once he recognized the roots of his coping mechanisms, and stopped judging himself for developing them, he could see that they were no longer serving him.

Tony took baby steps toward forming supportive relationships. He visited the yoga studio near his house and started showing up regularly for classes. He joined a surfing group. He rediscovered his passion for music and eventually learned to play the guitar.

As he learned to trust the in value of his relationships, Tony became less dependent on porn and more conscious of what he had to offer as a person. Over time, he went from looking at porn daily to going without it for weeks. Eventually, the fulfillment he felt from connecting with people in the real world helped him replace the temporary euphoria he got from the virtual world.

MOVING FROM BLAME TO ACCEPTANCE

Being aware of what happened in childhood and recognizing how your coping mechanisms impact your adult relationships is one of the keys to happiness and fulfillment. Forgiving your parents and/or your primary caregivers is an important part of this process.

Again, we all have imperfect parents/caregivers. After all, they came from imperfect parents, too. When you can make the transition from critiquing your caregivers and resenting them for their mistakes to accepting and humanizing them, you set yourself up for healthy relationships with friends and romantic partners in your adult life.

How do you make this transition? In part, it comes from understanding their perspective and knowing where they're coming from. In other words, your parents or your primary caregivers passed on to you whatever they experienced in their emotional environment growing up. Given their circumstances, they did the best they could.

At the same time, it's important to know that understanding your parents'/caregivers' perspective doesn't mean you have to deny your own pain. In childhood, if something goes wrong, we automatically think someone is to blame. In adulthood, we want to transition to an emotional space where understanding replaces blame, where we focus on cause and effect instead of right and wrong. Ultimately, the goal is to develop empathy for our caregivers and their imperfections as we hold on to empathy for ourselves and our own imperfections.

If you hold on to blame and anger toward your caregivers, your other relationships tend to suffer. This is what happened with Karine, whose story starts this chapter. Though she loved her boyfriend Henry, she was unconsciously taking out her anger with her parents on him.

As Karine reflected on what they'd dealt with as children, she realized her parents were repeating the only experience they knew. Both of them had grown up in abusive homes. Though she didn't feel ready to have a relationship with them, she learned to let go of some of her resentment. The more she released her anger toward them, the less that anger interfered in her relationship with Henry.

WHAT IF YOUR PARENTS/CAREGIVERS ARE DYSFUNCTIONAL?

As a therapist, I'm in favor of you maintaining a relationship with your parents/caregivers if you can. Why? Even if it's less than ideal, having a relationship with your caregivers puts you in a psychological space that makes it easier for you to form healthy relationships with other people.

But what if you come from a dysfunctional family? How do you have a relationship with your parents/caregivers and not hurt yourself in the process?

Maybe you have to separate from them for a while. Like Karine, sometimes you have to be angry with them and cut off contact with them in order to give yourself space to grow your self-esteem, recognize your coping mechanisms, and connect with your true self as you develop empathy for them.

In the meantime, it also helps to create secure attachments with other people. In a secure attachment, you strengthen your ability to hold on to your perspective and understand the person's perspective at the same time. This is an important emotional skill in any relationship, particularly in your relationship with your parents/caregivers.

WHEN TO LET GO

After years of being out of touch, Karine was ready to try again with her parents. She'd worked hard to recognize her coping mechanisms. She was making a conscious effort to move from an avoidant to a secure place in her relationship with Henry. She was doing her best to feel compassion for herself and for her parents.

Karine decided to meet her parents for lunch. At first, they seemed happy to see her. They told her how grateful they were to have her back in their lives and how amazing she was for getting her life on track.

But things deteriorated quickly. Toward the end of the meal, her father started to attack her. "You've always been manipulative and selfish," he said, "It's your fault we're not close. You just want me to give you money so you can get what you want."

Karine left in tears. "I can't have a relationship with them," she thought. "It's just too painful."

Ultimately, only you can decide whether it's possible to have a relationship with your parents/caregivers. The question to ask yourself is: Can you hold on to your true self and be in interaction with them? After that painful lunch with her parents, for Karine, the answer was "no."

After you establish that, it's important to ask yourself why. If you can't hold onto yourself, is it because you haven't built enough internal strength? Or is it because your parents/caregivers are stuck in their own pain loop and incapable of being emotionally close?

These questions can be tough to answer. Besides that, they can change over time. They certainly did for Karine.

RESETTING YOUR RELATIONSHIP WITH YOUR PARENTS/CAREGIVERS

As she grew older, Karine continued to work on strengthening her relationship with herself. Over time, as she built a fulfilling life—finding an accounting job she loved, creating a circle of supportive friends, and deepening her relationship with Henry—she realized she didn't need her parents anymore. That's when I encouraged her to get in touch with them again.

At first she didn't understand my logic. Why would she want to reengage with her parents when they'd caused her so much pain? "When you have to stay cut off from your parents to survive," I told her, "in some ways you're telling yourself that you're not strong enough to be in a relationship with them."

Now that she'd developed such a strong relationship with herself, I wanted her to feel her power to cope with anything and everything in her life, including her relationship with her parents.

The next time she met her parents for lunch, Karine cried— but this time her tears came from a place of relief instead of a place of pain. She went in with an attitude of empathy and emotional curiosity, and she came away with more knowledge and understanding about the pain her parents had gone through as children. For her, this was a major true self win.

These days, Karine has a different kind of relationship with her parents. Besides seeing each other once a month, they talk and text weekly. As an independent adult, she's closer to them than she ever could have been as a child—thanks to her relationship with herself, and to the other healthy relationships she learned to build in her life, including her friendships.

PRACTICE

Think back to your childhood. What false beliefs did you adopt about yourself in order to avoid seeing or feeling your parents'/primary caregivers' imperfections? Write them down in your journal.

For example, did you grow up believing you're not loveable? Not good enough? Not intelligent? Did you develop the belief that you're better than everyone else?

Once you've listed all your false beliefs about yourself, think about which one affects you most as an adult. Circle it.

Now reflect on the coping mechanisms you developed around that false belief. For example, if you believe you're not loveable, how did you adjust your behavior in ways to make yourself more loveable? Write down whatever coping mechanisms/behaviors come to mind.

Finally, ask yourself if you're carrying these behaviors into your adult relationships. Are you choosing to bring certain people into your life in order to replay the emotional injuries of the past?

If so, how can you step away from the unconscious patterns of childhood and bring yourself into the present? Whenever your present-day relationships trigger an emotional injury from the past, there are two things you can do:

Figure out what you need to say to yourself in order to come back to the moment. What words/thoughts can help bring you back to the emotional space of feeling the feelings that are happening right now? They can be something along the lines of: "It's okay to feel hurt, and it may seem like same the old story, but it isn't. This is now." Whenever you feel triggered, return to the words/thoughts that bring you back to your emotions in the present.

Look for evidence to the contrary. Though your loved one may be triggering you, they're hopefully not doing it intentionally, so it's important to look for evidence to support their good intentions in your relationship. Can you remember times when they looked at you with love in their eyes? Do they do things to make your life easier? Are they there when you need them? Try to be aware of their loving actions and behaviors. If you write them down, you can always come back to them whenever you feel triggered.

--- ⬆ ---

CHAPTER 10

HOW TO CREATE HEALTHY FRIENDSHIPS

I've been friends with Zoë since we were teenagers. In our teens and twenties, she liked to drink and party more than I did. Still, we always connected on a deep level whenever we spent time together one-on-one.

Toward the end of our twenties, Zoë transitioned out of her partying phase and focused on her career. Our friendship deepened. We saw each other almost every day. We went to the gym, to the movies, out to dinner. We studied together. We took weekend trips, staying up all night talking about anything and everything: our hopes and dreams, the people we were dating, the past, the future, the things that scared us.

Then I fell in love. Not long after that, I got deeper into meditation. Zoë and I started spending less and less time together.

Things came to a head one day when we were having lunch at my house. I can clearly picture us together in my kitchen, doing the dishes after we'd finished eating. I'd been telling her about all the new things that were happening in my spiritual practice and my relationship. She paused in the middle of stacking the plates in the cupboard. "I'm worried about you," she said. "You don't seem like yourself anymore."

I looked at her with what must have been hurt and disbelief, but she added: "...And I think maybe you're disappearing into your relationship."

She was right: I *was* disappearing into my relationship. And when I started meditating, I did feel a little disconnected from my old friends.

In that moment, though, I wasn't ready to hear what she was saying. Besides that, I couldn't see that her words were coming from her fear of losing me. I felt my face get hot. "I feel like you're not seeing me!" I yelled. "You of all people know how long I've waited to find someone to fall in love with. Why can't you just be happy for me?"

After that day, Zoë and I distanced ourselves. But we didn't end our friendship. We went from seeing each other almost every week to getting together every few months.

As time went by, Zoë and I continued to grow and change. I deepened my meditation practice. I started taking better care of my physical body. I grew my therapy practice. Zoë started studying meditation, too. She eventually trained to become a meditation teacher. She met someone she wanted to spend her life with. We became closer again.

After more than twenty years of friendship, Zoë and I are closer than we've ever been. Going forward, we may not always see eye to eye, but we've been through enough together to realize that we'll always have a strong connection. Ultimately, no matter what happens, we know our friendship will last.

WHY ARE FRIENDSHIPS IMPORTANT?

In the best cases, friendships allow us to experience feelings of acceptance, emotional intimacy, closeness, and love—without all the baggage and the challenges that often come with familial and romantic relationships.

In your familial relationships, you're part of a system of emotional processes that's been passed down for generations. As we discussed in chapter 9, realigning these emotional processes is one of the keys to feeling happier and more fulfilled in your life.

Your romantic relationships, which we'll explore in chapters 11 and 12, are an extension of the work you do in your familial relationships. What does this mean? Usually, when you're choosing a romantic partner, you pick someone who's in alignment with your family system, or you choose a person who pushes your buttons and compels you to look at unresolved issues from your family relationships—or you find someone who does both.

Friendships are different. Many of us, including many of my clients, are capable of having deep, meaningful friendships even as they struggle in their familial and romantic relationships. Why? You don't look to your friends to meet all your needs, as you might with a family member or a romantic partner. So your friendships can give you the freedom to practice acceptance and unconditional love; they can also be a place to heal, grow, and gather the strength to take on the deeper, more challenging issues you face in your life.

As I was coming out of depression and anxiety, my friendships became a crucial source of healing and support. By choosing to surround myself with people who accepted and respected my way of thinking, I was free to be who I was without worrying about any judgments or pain from the past. My friends made me feel totally understood in a way I had never felt before. Ultimately, they helped me own my feelings and connect with my true self, which also helped me realign my relationship with my parents.

WHAT CAN YOU EXPECT FROM YOUR FRIENDSHIPS?

Since many of us are entering into romantic relationships later in life, we often make unreasonable demands on our friends. However, if we want to have healthy friendships, the expectations we set for our friends should be different than for romantic relationships.

Since we're staying single longer, we often expect our friends to be everything to us. However, we don't have to choose friends who are perfectly compatible with us in every way. As I tell my clients, being friends with a diverse group of people, and learning to appreciate the different facets of each person, not only feels satisfying—it helps you grow.

You can have as many friends as you want. The key is to

surround yourself with people who accept you and whom you accept in return. Yes, you'll experience challenges and go through ebbs and flows in your relationships with your friends. In the end, though, your friendships are a place to feel good.

HOW TO MAKE FRIENDS

When you're making new friends, it often takes time to build a friendship that lasts. You're busy, other people are busy, and it can be challenging to find people you truly connect with.

Despite the challenges, making new friends is still worth the effort. Even if you're an introvert, and you enjoy spending time alone, you need other people to feel happy and fulfilled. In fact, according to a Harvard University study that spanned over seventy-five years, good relationships are the number one factor in creating a healthy, satisfying life.[18]

When I was letting go of anxiety and depression, I told myself I had a choice: either I could stay home and feel sad about not having friends, or I could take baby steps to create new relationships in my life.

I started by looking for group activities where I could do things I loved and connect with my true self. Though my negative mind discouraged me ("Oh, you don't want to go. You're not going to meet anybody anyway. Just go to the movies by yourself."), I pushed past it.

---

18 Curtain, Melanie. "This 75-Year Harvard Study Found the 1 Secret to Leading a Fulfilling Life." Inc. com. Accessed January 20, 2020. https://www.inc.com/melanie-curtin/want-a-life-of-fulfillment-a-75-year-harvard-study-says-to-prioritize-this-one-t.html.

Over and over, I put myself in situations where I could meet new people. I went online and signed up for things I was interested in. I went to a dodge ball meetup. I took an art class. I joined a women's surf group. Though I didn't automatically make friends, I was doing things that made me feel good. I was also starting to open up to people.

Though I was terrified, I eventually persuaded myself to join a group surf trip to Costa Rica. Before the trip, my stomach ached with dread. My negative mind went on and on about what a waste of time and money it was, and how uncomfortable I was going to feel. By then, I knew that negative mind voice well enough to know that it didn't have my best interests at heart. (If you need a refresher on how to recognize the voice of your negative mind, go back to chapters 3 and 4.)

I learned a lot about myself on that surf trip. I gained confidence. I met people who shared my passion for being outside and in the water. And I made a lifelong friend in the process.

If you're feeling lonely or feeling like something is missing in your social life, try signing up for group activities. Group experiences are a great way to fast-forward into sharing intimate experiences with other people, especially if you're bonding around a passion you have in common.

HOW TO CONNECT WITH PEOPLE

If you're in a social situation with a group of new people, how do you break the ice? One place to start is to find out what they're interested in and what you have in common.

Be curious. Ask questions: people love talking about themselves and feeling like someone is genuinely interested in getting to know them. Try to keep the balance between learning about the other person and talking about yourself as even as you can.

If you tend to talk a lot, make a conscious effort to draw out the other person. If you're someone who prefers to listen, try to contribute to the conversation more than you normally would. In other words, when you're engaging with someone new, work toward the opposite of your natural predisposition.

If you tend to feel self-conscious or anxious in social situations, try going into a room and observing people. Just like you, they're focused on themselves and probably feeling self-conscious. (As we discussed in chapter 1, most people feel awkward in social settings, especially with people they don't know, so you don't have to feel like you're the only one who's anxious.)

Think about what you would want to hear if you were feeling awkward. Wouldn't you appreciate it if someone approached you with warmth and confidence and paid you a compliment—or asked you questions to give you the space to open up? If you're not sure how to do this, try observing people with good social skills. My friend Zoë, for example, is great at engaging people in conversation. She comes across as self-assured, which makes people believe that she's someone worth getting to know. Besides that, she asks a lot of questions and listens carefully to people's answers. In the meantime, she shares things about herself that relate to what her conversation partners are saying.

Ultimately, when you pay less attention to your self-consciousness and focus on what other people are feeling, it becomes easier to connect with them.

SHOW YOUR VULNERABILITY

As you interact with new people, find a way to reveal something real about yourself. People are much more engaged when they feel like you trust them with something personal. For example, instead of saying something like, "Oh, yeah, I like that movie, too," try saying something introspective like, "I like that movie because it reminds me of this experience I had with my mom when I was a kid." When you share a deeper part of yourself, it helps build connections with people.

But when does sharing become over-sharing? How do you make sure you're not revealing too much too soon? When I'm sharing something real, I make sure it's something that's not currently affecting me in a way that feels raw or unprocessed. For example, I often tell people I was depressed in high school. Anybody can know about that part of my past because it's not who I am now. Sharing that detail says something about what I've overcome and who I've become. I often talk about being depressed in a first session with a client. If it's relevant, I mention it at parties, too.

The key to being vulnerable in social situations is to show people who you are without expecting them to take care of you. If you're sharing something intimate and feeling like you need someone to support you through it, it's better to discuss it with a close friend. However, when you share things with people that reveal a part of you that's already healed, you're communicating in a way that can lead to deeper connections.

BEWARE OF JUDGMENT

If we judge people too quickly, we miss the chance to make a potentially positive connection with them. I learned this lesson with Jasmine, who was one of my classmates in grad school. When I first met her, I found Jasmine extremely annoying. She asked so many questions in class that people would roll their eyes. Any time we were assigned an in-class activity, Jasmine would take over, bossing everyone around, being loud and abrasive.

Then Jasmine and I were assigned to a trainee-ship at the same school, where we worked as counselors for emotionally disturbed students. Every day we ate lunch together and discussed our cases. If something upsetting happened, we supported one other. If one of us had a challenging case, we looked at different ways to approach it.

The more time we spent together, the more I could see that Jasmine had a huge heart. She genuinely wanted to help those kids. At the same time, she respected me. She asked me for advice. She was generous with compliments.

As I got to know her, I realized that Jasmine's abrasiveness and anxiousness was rooted in her experience with her family—she was the oldest of six—and her culture (where she had to be assertive to be heard). Being bossy and talking a lot were things she did when she was nervous. The closer we got, the more I could tease her about them. Little by little, her walls came down, and I saw her true self. But I wouldn't have seen it had I not given her a chance.

As you're working to separate your negative mind from your true self (a concept we explored in chapter 4), it's important to do the same with everyone else. My experience with Jasmine taught me how powerful it can be to recognize when others' actions might be driven by their negative mind, and try to see their true self.

Had I gone with my initial judgment about Jasmine ("This woman is annoying. She's abrasive, and she asks too many questions. There's no way we're going to connect."), I would have missed out on a major emotional opportunity. Instead of dismissing her, I asked myself why she was pushing my buttons. As is usually the case in situations where we're triggered, it went back to a pattern from my childhood. In my family, it was "wrong" to be center stage, express big emotions, and talk more than listen. Getting to know Jasmine opened my eyes to this negative emotional pattern in my family—and being her friend was one of the things that helped me let go of it.

DON'T TAKE THINGS PERSONALLY

If you're in a situation where you don't have many friends and you're pursuing new friendships, it can be hard to understand when someone is being wishy-washy about your relationship. If someone acts ambivalent about making time for you, it's easy to take their behavior personally.

If you were cooler, if you were smarter, if you were more fun, then this person would want to spend time with you. And you'd have a ton of friends, right? This is how the negative mind likes to interpret other people's behavior. Just as you tend to blame yourself when your parents/caregivers make mistakes, it's easy to think it's somehow your fault when people don't want to spend time with you.

All of us make up stories about other people's behavior. We think we know the meaning behind it—but the truth is, we don't. Again, the reason people act the way they do usually goes back to their family history and their own unconscious patterns (which we explored in chapter 9)—or to the simple fact that they're leading busy lives.

When I met my friend Zoë, for example, she had hundreds of friends—and I had one. For the next few years, I initiated contact with her most of the time, but I didn't pressure her or make her feel bad when she didn't have time to get together or had to cancel.

Over the next few years, our contact gradually evened out, and Zoë sought me out as often as I got in touch with her. However, if I'd taken her lack of availability personally in the beginning, we never could have built the beautiful friendship we have now. In the meantime, I also pursued other friendships that didn't develop into anything deeper, but it didn't matter because I was exploring multiple options at the same time. That's the luxury of having lots of available time to socialize.

In any case, when you're working on building new friendships, it's important to remember that other people's behavior has nothing to do with you most of the time. When you can embrace this idea, it not only takes the pressure off your relationships, but it also helps you deepen your sense of self-acceptance.

APPRECIATE YOUR DIFFERENCES

The deeper you go in your friendships, the more likely you are to push your friends' buttons—and the more likely they are to push yours. Why? As you get closer to people, you start to raise your expectations and look to them to meet more of your needs. This isn't "wrong" or unhealthy—instead, it's a natural part of a relationship's evolution. Over time, your friendships sometimes grow to the point where they resemble family relationships.

As they deepen, your friendships can be an excellent training ground to practice healthy communication; they can actually help you prepare for more highly sensitive communication in your romantic and familial relationships.

Since the stakes are lower in your friendships than in your relationships with your family or romantic partners, the communication is less charged. This makes it much easier to communicate and give feedback from your true self.

If you're looking for ways to practice healthy communication with your friends, start with time, which we'll explore in the example below. In the context of friendship, time can be a "minor" issue that grows into a source of tension where we often misunderstand one another or hurt each other unintentionally.

TIME

What happens in a friendship when two people have a different sense of time? Let's look at the example of Erica and Rosa. My client Erica was getting increasingly frustrated with her best friend Rosa, who tends to over-schedule herself. "Every time I make plans with her to do something a couple of weeks in advance, she cancels at the last minute." Though they'd been friends for years, Erica was starting to feel angry every time she thought about Rosa: "Her behavior is just disrespectful, Jesse. Why should I bother?"

At some level, Erica thought Rosa was intentionally trying to hurt her. But what was underneath her anger?

"Well," Erica said, "If she really cared about me and valued me, she would show up. I just feel like I'm not important to her."

As someone who shows up on time and honors her commitments, I could identify with Erica. But at the same time, I wanted her to understand that Rosa's flakiness didn't reflect how much she cared. What about Rosa's work? What about her other relationships? Did she have trouble following through on her other commitments? The answer was yes.

People who are flaky or chronically late have their own reasons why they develop this behavior—and they usually go back to childhood. In Rosa's case, she came from a family where her parents lived on two coasts. She was constantly traveling back and forth. Nothing felt organized.

Knowing this about Rosa, I helped Erica realize that Rosa was unconsciously recreating the soundtrack from her childhood (as we discussed in chapter 9). She wasn't intentionally overscheduling herself. She was just accepting invitations from one thing to the next, until she reached the point where she felt like the kid who didn't have control of her time and was being pushed and pulled from coast to coast.

Once Erica understood that Rosa's sense of time was part of her unconscious pattern, she learned not to feel upset or disrespected when she canceled their plans. Instead of making her feel bad about her schedule and her ability to show up—which would have endangered their friendship—she taught herself not to take Rosa's behavior personally.

In the meantime, she stopped setting Rosa up to fail. Knowing that she wasn't going to change her relationship with time, Erica invited her to things where it mattered less if she canceled. If she wanted to go to a concert or a play, or reserve a table at a hot restaurant, she invited friends who would be more likely to show up. If she had a free afternoon or an invitation to a party, she invited Rosa. That way, if she canceled, Erica still enjoyed being on her own.

Ultimately, there's no right or wrong in this scenario. Since they had grown up differently, Erica and Rosa had each developed their own relationship with time. Though it was a different relationship, it didn't mean they couldn't be friends.

CONFLICT

As I wrote above, getting closer to people inevitably leads to conflicts and hurt feelings. All of us are dealing with the voice in the negative mind, so it's impossible not to be triggered at times. Still, my general rule for friendships is that they should involve as little anger as possible.

If you're getting angry with your friends because they're pushing your buttons, then it's important to figure out what's underneath that anger. If you want to be in a world where people are accepting and loving toward you, you have to give the same in return. In other words, sometimes you need to go inside yourself, as Erica did in the previous example, in order to repair your relationships.

Once you find the source of your anger—which in this case is usually connected to a fear of not being loveable or important—ask yourself whether you can work through it on your own (i.e., whether it touches on a past trauma and/or your family history).

If you can't work through it on your own (i.e., if it gets stuck or comes up over and over again), then express it. However, don't communicate until you're clear about the fact that your friend has good intentions and doesn't deliberately want to hurt you. (For more guidance on how to communicate when you're angry, go back to chapter 2.)

On the other hand, if you have a friend who's consistently angry with you and you don't reciprocate that anger, it's important to start the communication from a calm place. Try to understand what's triggering them. Make it clear that you want your friendship to be based on having good feelings and good intentions for one another.

Then allow your friend to tell you what's going on for them—

and know that it will probably be difficult to hear what they have to say. Whenever someone is giving us negative feedback or expressing how we've hurt them, our negative minds automatically start to catastrophize. We start to think things like, "Hey, this relationship isn't as safe as I thought," "I guess we're not as close as I thought," or "Maybe I'm a bad person." The truth is that most of us feel triggered when we're getting input about a situation where we've caused someone pain, especially if it's someone we care about.

In this situation, if we want the friendship to grow, it's important to push past the chatter in our negative mind. As scary and threatening as the conversation might feel, and as tempting as it might be to avoid it, we want to encourage our friends to communicate the emotions beneath their anger. Once we understand the source of their hurt feelings, then we can work on addressing them and understanding their perspective.

However, if you find yourself in a situation where a friend continues to get angry with you despite your efforts to understand where they're coming from, try to take a break from the conversation.

Over time, if they keep approaching you in anger, it might be time to take a break from the friendship for a while. Talk less. Spend less time together. Then see where you end up.

After all, you have enough relationship challenges with family and in your romantic life; you don't need to live in a state of anxiety about hurting your friends.

SUPPORTING FRIENDS IN A CRISIS

Though it might sound selfish, it's important to take care of your-self first when you want to support a friend who needs help. If you drop everything when they're upset, you run the risk of draining yourself and resenting them in the long run. Though it's tempting to go with them into crisis mode, it's important to continue doing the things in your life that make you feel good: get enough sleep, go to work or school, work toward your goals, exercise. This way, you actually set yourself up to give more to your friends. When you feel strong, happy, and recharged, you increase your capacity to offer support from a place of unconditional love.

To learn more about how to support the people in your life while still taking care of yourself, check out to this episode of my "Live Better" podcast: jesse-giunta-rafeh.com/podcast/2019/1/11/episode-3-bad-decisions

ACCEPT THE EBB AND FLOW

Finding the right amount of interaction with your friends can be tricky, especially when you're transitioning into adulthood. As you deal with all the changes happening in your life, it's natural for your friendships to ebb and flow.

As I wrote at the top of this chapter, my best friend Zoë and I are closer than we've ever been. Though it might seem like a contradiction, I think that closeness comes from having accepted the times when we needed to go off and explore on our own. When we were going through different stages of our development and valuing different things, we were willing to recognize that and give each other space.

This is the beauty of friendship. Being close to someone doesn't mean you have to constantly talk with them or spend time together. Your relationship can ebb and flow depending on what you need and where you are in your life.

When you don't have a strong sense of self-acceptance, the ebb phases of a friendship can feel personal and painful. It can be a challenge to internalize the idea that you're not having problems in your relationship when there's distance.

If you're feeling insecure or unhappy in the ebb phase of a relationship, it's important to look in the mirror. How much love and acceptance—or lack thereof—do you feel for yourself? The more you learn to accept yourself unconditionally, the more you can hold love in your heart for people regardless of how close they are to you. This is true for friendships, and it's true for romantic relationships as well—though it can be more challenging to deal with emotional distance in a romantic relationship, as we'll see in the next two chapters.

PRACTICE

What's one thing you need to work on in order to be a better friend? If you're not sure, think about which of your friends you could ask for feedback.

In the meantime, here are some examples. See which one(s) apply to you and commit to working on them for a certain period of time:

- Do you talk a lot more than your friends? If so, make it a point to spend time listening to them, asking good questions, and/or not interrupting when they're talking.
- Can you be vulnerable with your friends? If not, think about something that's important to you and choose a time and place to talk about it with someone you trust.
- Do you ask your friends for help? If not, the next time you're feeling overwhelmed or in need of support, reach out to them.
- Do you help your friends or look for ways to make their lives better?
- Are you judgmental about your friends? If so, what are you judgmental about? Think about ways you could be more accepting of your friends.

After a few weeks, reflect on how it feels to be a better friend. What was easy? What felt hard? What changes did you notice in your friendships? What changes did you notice in yourself?

CHAPTER 11

HOW TO ATTRACT THE RIGHT PARTNER

Sophia has a magnetic personality. Not only is she great at building deep friendships with different types of people, but she's also smart and creative. Besides getting admitted to a competitive Master's program at UCLA, she's landed coveted internships at companies with hundreds of other applicants.

When she first came to my office for therapy, Sophia believed in her intelligence and her ability to make friends. But she didn't believe that she was the kind of person who could attract a romantic partner.

Aside from her lack of experience, she wasn't confident in her physical body. She didn't think she looked like the kind of woman people would be attracted to—and she dressed and carried herself as though that were true. Though it was easy for her to make friends with men, she wasn't having any romantic success. She felt sad and frustrated.

As much as I understood Sophia's feeling that she had to be physically perfect, I wanted her to understand that, in spite of what she thought, and what society was telling her, appearance isn't the most important factor in finding a romantic partner.

I told her about my freshman orientation week at college, when my four hundred classmates and I got to know each other before classes started. As I talked with my classmates, I decided to do an experiment: I asked them who they were attracted to. Was it the most beautiful person in our class?

Over and over again, the same woman's name came up. I was surprised. She was definitely not the most attractive person in the class. And I was fascinated. What was it about her that made her so interesting to people? Over the next few days, I decided to pay more attention to her.

Here's what I noticed: this woman was completely in touch with her feminine energy. She walked, dressed, and talked with confidence. She seemed to believe in herself and her ability to connect with people. From that point on, I realized that it isn't our physical form that makes us attractive. It's what we believe about ourselves.

Over time, Sophia and I worked on building her belief that she was attractive. Being who she was, she had so much to offer. "You would be a kick-ass girlfriend," I told her. "You're going from one awesome event to the next. You're always surrounded by cool people, having a blast. You love music. You love to dance. The only thing missing is getting into your body and loving yourself."

Sophia asked a fashionable friend to help her buy some new clothes. She got a haircut that flattered her face. She started eating healthier and exercising more often, though she wasn't doing it to lose weight. She wanted to feel better in her own skin.

Over time, as she took care of her physical form in every way she knew how, Sophia started to appreciate herself—all of herself. Sure enough, men started to notice her. At first they just wanted to hook up with her. But before long, as her self-esteem went up, the quality of the men she attracted went up, too.

In the meantime, she continued going to concerts and exploring her love for music. At one of those concerts, she met James, a guitarist in a band she really liked. At first, he made it clear that he wasn't the type of person to commit. But the more Sophia talked to him, the more he could see how unique and special she was, and how magical their connection could be. As of this writing, Sophia and James have been together for over a year.

WHEN YOU FALL IN LOVE WITH YOURSELF, OTHER PEOPLE WILL, TOO

Once Sophia learned to fall in love with herself, it was natural for someone else to fall in love with her, too.

Her journey to meeting James echoes an idea I share with all my clients: You can only expect to feel another person's love as deeply as you love yourself.

So how do you fall in love with yourself? Just as you would

in any other romantic relationship: by dating yourself, which means you're not using dating apps or going out on dates with other people.

As weird as the idea might sound, if you're coming out of a breakup, feeling like you're stuck in a cycle of unhealthy relationships, or feeling hopeless about the idea of meeting someone, dating yourself is the best way to set yourself up for a healthy romantic relationship. Why?

When you date yourself, you start to feel alive and excited about your own life. Doing things like exploring your passions, renewing your commitment to school or your work, and spending time with your friends builds your connection with your true self. And when you're in your true self, you're not waiting for a romantic partner to come along and make you happy—because you already are. This is when you meet people who are attracted to the best version of who you are.

If your relationship circumstances aren't dire (that is, if you're not dealing with a breakup, you have some hope about your romantic prospects, and/or you're not falling into the same unhealthy relationship patterns over and over again), then it's possible to date yourself while you're dating other people.

Ultimately, the degree to which you abstain from other romantic relationships while you're dating yourself is up to you. However, if you want to enjoy the long-term benefits of this practice, it's important to be honest with yourself about where you are in your relationships, and what role they're playing in your life, when you make this decision. As I mentioned in chapter 6, sometimes we can't truly know how something is impacting us until we give it up for a while.

For my client Sarah, whose confidence and sense of self-worth were tied in with the men she dated, dating herself exclusively sounded unthinkable at first. After a breakup, she liked to rush into the next relationship. Instead of taking time to recover and reconnect with herself, she pursued people who embodied the things she thought her exes were lacking: "Shane was wrong for me," she said, after her last breakup, "He's too shy and awkward. I need someone more like Miles, who's incredible with people."

Over time, though, she realized Miles wasn't right for her either—and she started to feel frustrated about the prospect of ever meeting someone who was right for her. Her "grass-is-always-greener" approach to dating wasn't working, and she knew it. Before she could paint a clear picture of the person she wanted to be with, I told her, she needed to spend some time getting to know her adult self. So she decided to take a break from dating other people altogether.

As we'll see with Sarah's story, no matter where you happen to be in your romantic life, dating yourself exclusively increases your chances of creating a healthy relationship in the long run. Below are six steps to help you get started.

To get the maximum benefit from these steps, I strongly recommend that you journal every day, even if it's just a few lines. Write about what's hard, what feels fulfilling, and what you're learning about yourself and your passions. Journaling helps you internalize what you're experiencing and reinforce your connection with your true self.

- **Step 1:** Make a list of the strengths and good qualities you could bring into a loving relationship. Read this list every day to reinforce your positive feelings about yourself.

✎ **Step 2:** Make a list of all the things about you that present a potential problem with a future partner. Do you tend to get jealous? Is it hard for you to share your feelings? Have compassion for yourself around each item on this list, just as you would for a good friend. Then, coming from a place of love and acceptance, pick one thing to work on for a specific period of time and take baby steps toward improving it. If you're shy, for example, make it a goal to start conversations with people you meet in your daily life. The more you work on your weak spots, the more you release your fear about bringing them into future relationships.

✎ **Step 3:** As you open up to the possibility of love, set the goal to become the best version of yourself. When your negative mind kicks in ("Oh, it's never going to happen to me!"), redirect your focus to the positive parts of yourself and to developing your passions. What are you interested in? Do you have a creative project? What are your goals and dreams? Take yourself on dates, like going to lunch at a fun new restaurant, or spending an afternoon at the movies or at an art exhibit. Make time to do things that inspire you, whether it's going to a yoga class, starting an art project, or reading a new book. When you spend time pursuing the things you care about, you not only strengthen your belief that you have something to offer. You also reinforce the connection with your true self.

✎ **Step 4:** Stay connected to your friends. As I wrote in

the friendship chapter, your friendships are a source of comfort and happiness; they help you develop feelings of self-acceptance. They also offer a great opportunity to practice healthy communication, serving as a kind of training ground for more emotionally challenging relationships.

- ✔ **Step 5:** Take care of your body. You're not trying to fulfill some impossible media-driven ideal. However, like, Sophia, when you eat well and exercise, you start to feel better in your own skin and develop an appreciation for your body. (Go back to chapter 5 for specific tips on how to take good care of your physical body.)

- ✔ **Step 6:** Put some energy into your physical appearance. Sophia wanted someone to accept her exactly as she was—and she was a casual person who liked wearing sweat pants. But as she was meeting new people, she realized they knew nothing about her and what she had to offer beyond a brief interaction. People assumed if she didn't care about her appearance, she probably didn't care about the other aspects of her life, which was completely untrue.

If dealing with your appearance is a challenge, don't be afraid to ask for help. Ask a fashionable friend to go shopping with you to spruce up your wardrobe. If you admire the way one of your friends does their hair, ask them to help you with yours. Though they may seem superficial, paying attention to these details builds your confidence.

HOW DO YOU KNOW WHEN YOU'RE READY?

"How long is this going to take?" Sarah asked me. When I advise clients to date themselves before they start dating other people, this is usually their first question.

Though it's hard to put a timeline on it, it generally takes at least six months to a year to create an amazing life for yourself before you're ready to date other people. "Six months?!" Sarah said, "There's no way I can do that."

From where she was sitting, six months seemed long and impossible. At first, it felt difficult and lonely. But then something happened when she started to spend time doing things that felt fulfilling and inspiring to her—whether it was starting an art project, reading a new book, or hanging out with her friends—instead of going through dating apps. After a while, she felt a switch flip.

After six months, Sarah was actually afraid to start dating because she didn't want to lose the sense of fulfillment she had created in her life. She had never felt so good about herself, so loved. "That's how we know you're ready," I told her. "Instead of looking for someone to give you what's missing, you've given it to yourself. And now you want to protect it."

Sarah was technically ready to start dating other people at that point. But before she re-entered the dating world, I wanted her to take one more step to reinforce her feelings of self-love. Now that she'd learned to build a life that felt happy and fulfilled, I wanted her to see if she could stay in it for a few months on her own.

Before she turned on the dating apps, I wanted her to hold

on to herself just a little longer. Why? The deeper her connection to the best version of herself, the easier it would be to access when she was in a relationship.

And that's where Sarah is now. After a few false starts, she met Neel, who's as passionate, thoughtful, and adventurous as she is. Not only is their relationship close and meaningful, but it also gives her the space and strength to be her true self—which is what she'd been searching for all along.

EXPAND YOUR SOCIAL WORLD

Once you've fallen in love with yourself, you're ready to enter the dating world. What's the best way to approach it? Though not very romantic, the truth is that finding your ideal partner is actually a numbers game. You're much more likely to meet your match when you put yourself in a diversity of locations with a diversity of people.

Try to say "yes" to every invitation, even if it's not something you would normally do. Take classes on topics you're interested in. Sign up for online dating.

As I wrote in chapter 10, choosing activities that interest you helps you connect with your true self, making it easier to open up and meet people.

For example, when I signed up for a group surf trip to Costa Rica, I not only made friends. For the first time in my life, I experienced what it felt like when multiple people were attracted to me. Why did this happen? Because I was in my element.

Being outside and surfing for six hours a day was exciting and thrilling. I felt completely happy and fulfilled. Though I didn't join the trip with the intention of meeting a potential partner—in fact, *because* I wasn't intending to meet a potential partner—people were drawn to me. All of a sudden there was an attractive lawyer from New York and a surf instructor vying for my romantic attention. Throughout the trip, I also felt others in our group being attracted to my energy and wanting to be around me.

When you decide you're ready to date, the key is to show up with the goal to simply have fun and connect to new people. If you're in a new social situation, don't just talk with people you're interested in romantically. Try to connect with everyone. First of all, you can never have too many friends. Secondly, you might meet someone who introduces you to someone else you have chemistry with.

MIRROR AND MATCH

As you're meeting potential partners, making an effort to match their energy increases the odds that they will open up to you. This isn't a manipulative exercise. Mirroring and matching actually helps other people feel more comfortable in your presence, enabling you to connect more deeply.

For example, my client Rebecca is a person full of love, life, and positivity; she's also loud and hyper. Before she learned to mirror people, she entered every room like a marching band. No matter who was there, no matter what the general mood was, her first words were usually something like, "Isn't today beautiful?"

Sometimes people found her refreshing. But if they didn't share her positive energy, they often felt like she was on a different plane. Over and over, she unintentionally pushed people away.

She knew she had to change her approach. When she entered a room, she started to pay attention to the "music" people were giving off. If it was a slow song, she relaxed. If it was a techno beat, she shifted into her natural high-energy mode. By approaching her encounters like a dance, and mirroring the rhythm of the people she met, she started to create deeper connections with them.

SHARE YOUR BEST PARTS

As you meet new people, your interactions with them will usually be brief. As much as you want to mirror and match their energy, it's also important to focus on sharing the best parts of you.

This isn't about hiding your pain or limiting yourself to only sharing the positive. However, when you're in a situation online or at a party where you can only share so much about yourself, you want to do it from a place that demonstrates a degree of love for your life.

When you're introducing yourself to someone, you want to focus on things that you're passionate and excited about. Maybe it's a hobby like cooking or rock climbing. Maybe it's a class you're taking, or a project you're working on. Maybe it's someone you're close to in your family, or a friend you care deeply about.

Sharing your passions and your excitement about life lights people up. It also increases the possibility that they'll want to spend more time with you, giving you the opportunity to show more of who you are.

If you don't want to, you don't have to focus exclusively on the positive. However, if you're meeting people and immediately saying things like "my mom is so annoying" or "I come from an abusive family," you want to back up those statements with a redemption story. As I mentioned in chapter 10, showing your vulnerability and sharing the challenging parts of your life can help create genuine connections. The key, though, is to focus on things you've already worked through, especially when you're meeting someone for the first time.

When you're meeting new people, sharing the best parts of you isn't about being someone you're not. The truth is—and I speak from experience—you have an extremely limited amount of time, especially in the world of online dating, so the goal is to bring the best version of yourself to your interactions. If you're making an effort to look your best, why not focus on the most impressive parts of your life, too?

If you're reading this and feeling like you don't have anything exciting or admirable in your life to share with potential partners, consider taking a break from dating other people. Commit to dating yourself for a set period, taking the time and space to go through the steps I outlined at the beginning of this chapter. By building the connection with your true self, you're much more likely to meet someone who appreciates—and brings out—the best parts of you.

ADOPT AN ATTITUDE OF ABUNDANCE

As you enter the dating world, it's easy to become overly attached to the idea that a certain person is the only person for you—and that you'll never be happy unless they choose you.

However, there are two problems with this way of thinking. One, if it feels like your life depends on a certain person liking you, it puts so much pressure on the situation that you can't be yourself with them. Two, you blind yourself to who the person actually is.

My client Olivia often felt this way. One day, she was suffering from a crush so strong she couldn't think about anything else, so she scheduled an emergency session with me.

"As soon as I like someone," she said, "I become obsessed with them. It takes over every fiber of my being."

I told her she wasn't alone. "I'm guessing a lot of your friends are having the same experience," I said. "But that's not love."

It's easy to confuse obsession and heightened emotions as a sign that a certain person is meant for you. However, when you're intensely fixated on someone, you're not actually trying to connect with them—you're looking to fill a void in yourself.

As I told Olivia, if you're stuck in an obsessive place, it helps to believe that if a relationship is meant to be, and a certain person is your person, you'll end up together simply by being you. It won't happen if you force it.

Genuine attraction isn't always instantaneous. The truth is, it can take time for your true self to connect with the other person's true self—and this is the connection you need in order to figure out whether you're a good fit for each other.

How do you allow this connection to happen? Instead of obsessing about details and trying to interpret the other person's behavior (e.g., "Why didn't they text me back?" "When are they going to set up our next date?"), focus on bringing the best version of yourself to the table.

Ask yourself: Are you taking care of yourself physically, eating well, and exercising? Are you pursuing your passions? How connected do you feel with your friends? When you realign yourself with what you're grateful for in your life, it becomes easier to let things unfold organically with potential partners. You create space for your potential partner to be your *partner*, not your healer.

In the end, as I told Olivia, when someone is into the best version of you, you'll know. The energy will be clear. You won't be wondering where you stand. You won't need to manipulate this or negotiate that. If it's the right person for you, the attraction will be there—it's not something you have to create.

PRACTICE PATIENCE

When you're entering the dating world, practicing patience goes hand in hand with having an attitude of abundance. For most of my twenties, I was single. Sometimes I was afraid I would never find someone or have the experience of being in love. I confused my fear with loneliness, thinking I was in pain because I didn't have a partner.

One day, as I was trying to process my disappointment after yet another bad date, a question popped into my mind: "If you knew right now that in a year you were going to meet the person of your dreams, would you still be in pain at this moment?" The answer was "no." Every time I started feeling sad about my love life, I asked myself this question. The answer was always "no."

The more you can internalize the idea that you have time for multiple romantic experiences, and the more you can learn to enjoy being single, the more likely you are to attract the right partner. Instead of projecting over-eagerness and desperation, which turn people off, you start to radiate confidence and wholeness that draws people in.

Whenever you don't feel empowered and confident, try deactivating your dating profile for a while. Go back to connecting with yourself.

This is what I did when I was single: when I felt centered and excited about my life, and interested in meeting people for the sake of meeting people, I activated my profile and showed up to parties. When I couldn't access that confidence and fulfillment, I went back to dating myself, spending time with my friends and doing things that made me happy.

I spent years going in and out of the online dating world, fluctuating between fear and self-acceptance. By the time I met the love of my life, I was ready. By practicing patience and not rushing into a relationship, I'd developed a loving relationship with myself in the meantime.

STAY OPEN

You can't necessarily tell who a person is from one inter-action. In the online dating world, it's easy to make snap judgments and close the door too quickly on people who could potentially be a good match for you.

When my client Selena was starting out with the online dating, she came to my office one day feeling frustrated about a phone call she'd tried to set up with someone she'd met online.

"We planned to talk around seven," she said. "I decided to lock myself in my dad's office a little before seven, to get a little privacy from my family. At seven-fifteen, I came out. At seven forty-five, I texted him that I didn't hear from him and hoped he was okay. About eight, he texted me back to ask if I was ready to talk. I just felt frustrated and annoyed. Is that normal?"

Her reflex was to rule out this person because he didn't share her sense of time. Though I could understand why she was upset, I didn't want her to take his behavior per-sonally—and I didn't want her to close the door on the idea of meeting him.

Who we are online isn't always who we are in reality. And, as I wrote in chapter 10, our relationship with time is rooted in our family history and the emotional soundtrack we experienced as we grew up. So it's important to stay open, give people the benefit of the doubt, and let them show you who they are before you rule them out.

WHAT ABOUT SEX?

In today's dating culture, there's an immense amount of pressure to have sex quickly and casually. Though I'm not judging anyone based on how fast they have sex—all of us have the right to create our own sexual boundaries—treating sex like it's no big deal can lead to problems.

Maybe you understand the concept of free love and casual sex intellectually, but your body doesn't. When you have sex, you release hormones that make you feel more connected to the other person than you might be in reality. This can get very confusing, especially for women.

How does this confusion play out when you have sex? Let's look at the experiences of my clients Kim and Aaron.

KIM

Like her friends, Kim was drawn to the idea of being sexually free. Whenever she went on a date, she usually ended up having sex. She liked feeling physically close, connected, and taken care of. Sometimes it even gave her a high.

"I'm a person who likes to have sex," she told me. "And I can have sex casually."

But when her dates didn't contact her afterward, or want to be in a relationship with her, she felt hurt and anxious. Still, she tried to rationalize her emotions: "I'm fine," she told herself, "It's no big deal." Then she would meet someone else and have sex with them, hoping it would lead to more.

Like a lot of young women, Kim thought saying "no" to

sex meant she wasn't free. If the rest of her generation was having sex, why couldn't she? On top of that, if she refused to have sex, she was afraid to miss an opportunity to be with someone great.

This was a belief rooted in her low self-esteem. If someone truly wanted to be with her, they would wait as long as it took. If a potential partner disappeared after she said "no," then she never had their interest in the first place.

Ultimately, I didn't tell Kim to stop practicing free love and having casual sex. But I did ask her to evaluate how she felt after sex. Was she enjoying the act itself and still feeling good about it the next day? Or was she having the experience and feeling sad and anxious afterward?

AARON

When he was in high school, Aaron was overweight, pimply, and immature. He was also socially awkward and extremely shy. To him, sex was as terrifying as it was impossible.

After he graduated high school, Aaron blossomed. He grew a few inches. He started working out. His skin cleared up. He got serious about his studies. He matured in every way. For the first time in his life, girls were interested in him. And, he realized he could have sex with them.

"Jesse, it's amazing," he said. "I can go to a party and hook up with a girl, and I'm having all these experiences. It's awesome!"

But before long, he started to feel bad. "The girls say it's okay, whatever happens. But it doesn't really seem like it's okay," he said. "I just feel like their expectations and my expectations aren't in alignment, and I'm hurting their feelings over and over again."

He was right. Regardless of what they were telling him, those girls were letting him into their bodies. "As much as they'd like it to be true that you don't have to be their friend or date them," I told him, "it doesn't feel good to them when you don't want to talk to them afterward."

Though it wasn't an easy choice, ultimately Aaron decided he didn't want to have sex with people he wasn't dating. Not having contact with his sex partners afterward didn't bother him—what was painful for him was seeing how he was hurting their feelings.

WHY WAIT TO HAVE SEX?

In today's dating world, especially in the online dating world, things move at hyper-speed: You're supposed to know right away whether you like someone—and have sex right away, too. If you do anything that's remotely unattractive, then people disappear. How can you find a potential mate if you're under so much pressure to rush things?

You might think I'm old-fashioned, but I believe the best way to build a great relationship is to take it slow. When you're dating someone who has the potential to be your partner, you have a better chance of building a healthy relationship if you practice patience. Instead of going straight to sex and romance, try connecting with them on a friendship level first. Even if the attraction is there, you don't need to be having sex. Why?

Sex is the most vulnerable, connected thing you can do. Being that close to someone before you decide whether or not you want to be in a relationship with them clouds your ability to see who they are—and how you connect with them emotionally. While a powerful sexual connection feels amazing, it can make you seem more compatible with someone than you actually are.

On top of that, when you've worked to develop your connection with your true self, it can be challenging to hold on to that connection if you sleep with them too soon. If you're having sex with someone, because of the closeness you feel, it's tempting to lean on them to help you cope with things you previously dealt with on your own.

If you want to create a healthy romantic relationship, try to wait until you're ready to commit before you have sex. You don't have to marry the person or be with them for the rest of your life. However, when you wait until you're emotionally committed, sex feels more like the intimate act that it is. At the same time, you hold on to yourself—which is the key to building a relationship that lasts. In chapter 12, we'll explore how to sustain a healthy romantic relationship.

PRACTICE

Below are three steps you can take toward attracting the right partner. You're free to determine the size of the baby step you take here. If step one is all you can manage right now—great! Start there, and once that feels easy and you're ready for the next challenge, move on to steps two and three.

Step 1: Create a list of the strengths and good qualities you have to offer in a relationship. Read this list every day.

Step 2: From a place of love and self-acceptance, make a list of the things about you that might present a challenge with a future partner. If you can't figure out your blocks, ask someone you trust about something you might want to work on.

Step 3: Pick one thing about yourself that you want to improve and choose one thing you'll do over a specific period of time to address it. If you don't feel good about your physical body, commit to moving in your favorite way three times a week, or take time to focus your attention on a part of your body you like when you get out of the shower. If you have a hard time opening up to people, make a point of volunteering something about your day to every person you interact with.

As you feel ready, commit to choosing other parts of yourself you want to work on and take baby steps toward improving them.

Along the way, record your feelings in your journal. How does each step feel? Most importantly, continue to give yourself credit for staying on a path to growth and self-love.

CHAPTER 12

HOW TO SUSTAIN A HEALTHY ROMANTIC RELATIONSHIP

Liam was the kind of man my client Charlette always dreamed of being with. He was attractive, wealthy, came from a great family, and had a successful career and a big group of close friends he always made time for.

Liam was deeply attracted to Charlette, and they quickly became a couple. As time went by, they learned more about each other, discovering that they both suffered from depression. Initially, this realization brought them closer.

Charlette started turning to Liam whenever she got depressed. She wanted him to take care of her. Because of the way they felt about each other, she thought he could make her feel better. It worked at first. But after a while, no matter what he did, Liam couldn't cheer her up anymore.

When he couldn't change how she felt, it made him feel like less of a man. It also triggered his own depression. So he stepped back. He tried less. Before long, Charlette felt like he wasn't doing enough.

DEPENDENCE AND LOVE

Like Charlette, we all depend on our partners to some degree. That's part of having a partner, isn't it? It feels great to be with someone who (hopefully!) sees you as the most amazing person on the planet, who boosts your confidence, calms your anxiety, and eases your depression.

As wonderful as that reinforcement feels, though, it's similar to having training wheels on a bike. Once you enter into a romantic relationship, it's easy to start relying on your partner to feel confident—as easy as it is to depend on those training wheels holding you up.

As I wrote at the end of chapter 11, when you finally find the person you've been searching for, it's almost instinctive to count on them for validation and love. We all do it. However, we need to be careful about how much we do it.

When you start relying on your partner as your coping mechanism for a sustained period of time, it not only puts a strain on your relationship, it also causes you to lose touch with your ability to create your own happiness.

If you want to avoid leaning on your partner too much—and sustain your relationship in the long-term—the key is to figure out when you're in a space of dependence versus a space of love. How can you tell the difference?

When you expect your partner to fill a need inside you, as

Charlette did, you're in a space of dependence. When you want them to express their love in a certain way, tell you how great you are on a regular basis, act a particular way around family or friends, or base their life decisions on what you want, you're also in a space of dependence.

Love is different. When you're in a space of love, you find joy in your partner, who they are, and what they're passionate about. It doesn't matter what they do. When you feel love for them, they don't need to change in any way.

Having a successful romantic partnership doesn't mean you always have to be in a space of love; that's just not realistic. In a committed relationship, you constantly fluctuate between love and dependence. However, the more you can hold on to yourself, the more you create a space of love.

THE RECIPE FOR A SUCCESSFUL RELATIONSHIP

Over years of helping clients navigate their romantic relationships, and learning to be in a healthy relationship of my own, I've pared down the recipe for a successful relationship to four main ingredients:

1. Fulfill your own needs as much as you can.

2. Accept everything you can about your partner.

3. What you can't accept, communicate to your partner with love.

4. Acknowledge your partner when they change to meet your needs.

Let's explore each ingredient and break down its components.

Once you choose someone you want to commit to, it's important to focus on being the best partner you can be without sacrificing yourself. When you hold on to your own goals and dreams, you create a source of fulfillment that belongs to you. In other words, your partner isn't the only thing in your life making you happy.

The thing that causes many relationships to fall apart is letting go of the reins of building self-confidence. As soon as you hand that job over to your partner, or start depending on them to make you feel good, you become less attractive. People fall in love with people who are self-assured and have their own sense of purpose.

When I feel myself relying on my husband Mark to make me feel better, I know it's a sign that I need to refocus on making myself feel better. I make more time for my friends. I take long walks. I do some extra yoga sessions. Even though I don't tell him what I'm doing, he responds every time: "Oh, my gosh, you're the most beautiful woman," he'll say, "I'm so in love with you."

Why does this happen? When I refocus on myself, I'm resetting the connection with my true self. Whether or not he's conscious of it, Mark can always feel that shift.

Know How Your Past Affects the Present

Another aspect of fulfilling your own needs in a relationship is being aware of how you might be projecting your emotional past onto the present. As I wrote in chapter 9, all of us grow up with a unique emotional soundtrack and a certain level of emotional intimacy, which we unconsciously re-create in our adult relationships.

The more clarity you have about your emotional history, and what your triggers are, the less likely you are to bring negative emotional patterns into your adult relationships. When you recognize what you're bringing with you from childhood, it's easier to distinguish the things you're upset about in your relationship from the things you're unconsciously doing to push your partner away.

If you're not aware of your emotional patterns, you run the risk of sabotaging your relationships. To learn how to address the emotional patterns of your past, please revisit chapter 9.

THE SECOND INGREDIENT: ACCEPT EVERYTHING YOU CAN ABOUT YOUR PARTNER

The second ingredient in the recipe for a successful relationship is to accept everything you possibly can about your partner. Once you commit to someone, it's important to love them for who they are instead of constantly trying to change them.

At some point in your life, you've probably heard the serenity prayer: "God, grant me the serenity to accept the things I cannot change, the courage to change the things

I can, and the wisdom to know the difference." You can apply this prayer to relationships, too—especially romantic relationships.

So how do you get to a place of accepting your partner for who they are—and understanding the difference between what to accept and what to address in your relationship? It starts with understanding that there is no perfect partner. In spite of what our culture tells us, in spite of what we've internalized from Disney movies and romantic comedies, the perfect partner doesn't exist.

If you're feeling upset about your partner doing X, Y, or Z, it's tempting to think they have to change in order for you to feel better. If your partner shows up late or doesn't clean their dishes right away, the negative mind kicks in, trying to convince you that your partner's behavior is a sign of something wrong in the relationship.

However, as I wrote in chapter 10, when someone does something that upsets you, it's important to remember that you don't know the meaning behind their behavior (though you think you do).

When I want to address an issue in my relationship with Mark, for example, I hold in my heart the fact that he loves me and would never want to upset me. Instead of coming at it from the perspective that he's wrong, or that he needs to pay for his mistake, I look at his behavior as a miscommunication or an unintentional action that's somehow pushed my buttons. In other words, I know he's not trying to hurt me.

When you can hold on to the idea that your partner has

good intentions and accept them for who they are, it's much easier to address the issues that are truly worth addressing over the course of your relationship. If your partner is behaving in a way that doesn't feel good to you, you want to respond to that behavior from a place of love, holding an attitude of hope that things can change for the better.

Time, Dirt, and Money

When it comes to accepting your partner, it can be especially challenging when it comes to things like time, dirt, and money.

All of us have relationships with time, dirt, and money that are comparable to our relationships with other human beings—and they're based on our upbringing. If your ideas around time, dirt, and money don't align with your partner's, it can create distance and conflict in your relationship.

Time

In chapter 10, we explored how different ideas around time can impact friendships. The stakes are even higher in romantic relationships. If you're someone who shows up on time and your partner is consistently late, or vice versa, time is something you need to negotiate because it can have a big impact on your life.

However, when you discuss time with your partner, you want to treat it as a logistical issue rather than a 911 emergency. Instead of catastrophizing the issue or approaching it from a place of anger or righteousness (e.g., "If you respected me, you'd be on time."), it's important to look at where you and your partner are coming from with respect to time.

How did your family handle time? How did your partner develop their relationship with time as they were growing up? In this scenario, the goal isn't to figure out who's right and who's wrong—it's about understanding the deeper meaning behind your behavior and finding a solution that works for both of you from a place of acceptance and love.

How does this work in practice? You might say something to your partner along these lines: "Hey, babe, it would mean a lot to me if we could work on figuring out a way to be more on time. I know it's not how you grew up, but it's how I grew up, and now it makes me anxious every time we're late when we go somewhere. Can we try to figure something out together? Can we come up with a system where it doesn't feel like I'm nagging you, but where I don't have to be anxious?"

Dirt

Dirt is another issue that can stir up our emotions in a romantic relationship. If you grew up in a clean household and your partner in a messy one, it can lead to arguments that come up again and again. If your partner tends to leave their clothes on the floor or doesn't clean up after themself in the kitchen, it often brings up resentment or even anxiety.

If you and your partner have an issue with dirt, it's important to approach it without judgment. You were raised in a family that taught you XYZ. Your way isn't the "right" way; it just comes from the beliefs you developed in childhood.

The key is not to judge your partner for having different beliefs and a different history. Their behavior isn't a reflection of their feelings about you. Approaching your partner with this awareness is a healthy starting point to work through your differences.

Money

Even if you differ from your partner when it comes to time and dirt, I have high hopes that you can negotiate a solution that works for both of you. With money, however, it can be challenging if your values don't align at least somewhat.

I've seen money become a point of conflict in many of my clients' relationships. Sharee and Ash are one example: Sharee is very future-focused and constantly saving money. Meanwhile Ash likes to focus on the present, bouncing from one fun experience to the next. Though he still pays his half of the bills, he's not saving for the future.

"He's irresponsible," Sharee said during one of our couple's sessions. "If he valued me, then he'd be setting us up for the future."

Ash sees things differently: "She's trying to control everything about me," he said. "My money and my free time."

Who's right and who's wrong in this scenario? Neither one of them. Sharee and Ash just have different financial value systems. Neither one is right or wrong, good or bad. If you look at their approach to money on a continuum, with present-focused Ash on one end and future-focused Sharee on the other, they're just very far apart.

If money is an issue in your romantic relationship, the first way to address it is to figure out where you and your partner come down on the financial continuum. Are you on the future-focused/frugal end? Is your partner a present-focused free spirit?

If you're not on the same financial page, ask yourself this: Are you close enough on the continuum to understand the other person's perspective? Just as important: Are you open to negotiating and learning from your partner's approach?

If you think you might be on either extreme of the money continuum, I encourage you to go back to chapter 8 and take a closer look at your relationship with money.

Integrating Your Partner into Your Life

As you integrate your partner into your life and relationships, it's important to keep accepting them for who they are. However, that acceptance can be challenging if your partner doesn't get along with other people who are important to you.

Being single for most of my twenties, I was used to relating to people on my own and deciding how close to people I wanted to be. However, when Mark came into my life, I was no longer the only one in control of my social interactions. When I introduced him to my friends, I was afraid of how his behavior might reflect on me.

Mark relates to people differently than I do. He likes to tease. He also loves playing devil's advocate. For him, listening to people defend their opinions is a fun intellectual exercise. At first, my friends didn't understand his humor at all. "Who is this guy?! We can't tell when he's serious and when he's kidding."

That's when I realized how complicated it can be to introduce your romantic partner into your life. What if my friends couldn't get along with him? I struggled with anxiety about the way things were unfolding between them.

Over time, I decided to hold on to the idea that I love Mark, and I love my friends. I tried to have faith that they would figure out how to come together. I didn't have to control the situation to make it work. I believed they could all be part of my life.

Ultimately, I realized that I wasn't responsible for Mark's relationships with my friends and family—and vice versa. By constantly worrying about how other people in my life were relating to him, and whether he was doing a good job representing us as a couple, I was not only creating stress for myself. I was also running the risk of making him feel self-conscious and lose confidence in who he is.

Besides that, I realized that the more stressed out I acted about my friends not liking Mark, the more I validated the idea that they needed to protect me. In other words, if I were acting anxious or stressed with Mark around my friends, they would assume he was the cause—and resent him for it. In the end, I would create what I feared.

Though the process took time, and I continued to feel some anxiety along the way, my friends grew to accept, appreciate, and eventually love Mark. In the end, what they wanted most for me was to be with someone who made me happy and took good care of me—and he was doing just that. Over time, the more they could see how much joy he brought to my life—and the more I let go of the need to engineer our interactions—the more they understood why I chose to be with him (and the more they liked being around him).

Trust

Once you've chosen to commit to someone, another important aspect of accepting everything you can about them is learning to trust them. This means not reading their text messages, not looking at the search history on their computer, and not questioning them about cheating on you. If you want a healthy romantic relationship that lasts, trust is fundamental.

If something is holding you back from trusting your partner, it can mean one of two things: either you've picked the wrong person, or you have trust issues rooted in trauma from your past.

How can you tell the difference? Focus on your partner's actions. If they behave in ways that betray your trust, then they don't deserve it. However, if you know your inability to trust has something to do with your past, it's important to work through those issues on your own. How?

Seek help from friends you trust, try therapy, and/or work on building your faith that you're a loveable partner. (To learn more about developing your sense of self-love, return to chapter 11.)

Jealousy

If your partner is trustworthy and you're still having trust issues, it's often because you don't believe you're valuable or lovable.

If you often feel jealous, or if jealousy is something you experience in all of your relationships, you may have a hard time internalizing the idea that you're capable of having a loving relationship. You can trace this pattern back to an emotional injury in your past.

Instead of running to your partner when you're feeling jealous, try to figure out what you're actually afraid of. Sometimes it's a deeply rooted trauma. But often it's an overwhelming general feeling that you're not good enough or loveable enough.

Once you establish your root fear, question it. How do you know you're not good enough? Why did this person want to be with you in the first place? What do they like about you? You can also approach it in a more general way: what makes you a good partner?

If you're having a hard time answering these questions, ask your friends and loved ones. Since they're not directly involved in your romantic relationships, they can give you valuable feedback that's sometimes easier to hear than the feedback from your partner. Ultimately, the people in your life are there to be real with you and to support you (which can also make them feel good).

Though it's tempting to share your feelings with your partner when you're feeling jealous, I don't recommend it. By looking to them for validation, you're basically telling them you don't think you have enough value for them. This is the last thought you want to instill in someone you have strong feelings for.

However, I'm not saying you shouldn't ever seek out your partner for reassurance or support. I am saying it can be unhealthy if it becomes a compulsive loop. If you run to your partner every time you feel insecure, you might feel better in that moment, but that feeling doesn't last. When you go back to your partner again and again, their reassuring words start to lose their impact over time. Why? Because the insecurity is rooted in you, not the relationship. In other words, your partner can't change something you've internalized. Only you can.

THE THIRD INGREDIENT: WHAT YOU CAN'T ACCEPT, COMMUNICATE TO YOUR PARTNER WITH LOVE

After you've worked through all the things you can accept about your partner, communicate whatever you can't accept with love.

However, before you decide *what* you want to communicate to your partner, you want to be aware of *how* you communicate with them.

At the beginning of your relationship, you and your partner set up your communication patterns and ways of dealing with disagreements. If you get into the habit of communicating in anger, by calling each other names and swearing, for example, it can do long-term damage to your relationship. If you're mean to one another when you fight, it's something you definitely want to address. (For tips on how to deal with anger, especially when it comes to communication, return to chapter 2.)

Aside from calling each other names or being mean to one another, sometimes we punish our partners by giving them the silent treatment. To clarify: when I say silent treatment, I don't mean taking an hour to cool off before you can have a difficult conversation from a calm place. In relationships, the silent treatment means withdrawing your love with the intention of making your partner feel the pain you're feeling, which makes them anxious and upset. This is a dynamic you want to address right away because it can also affect your relationship in the long-term.

Once you're aware of how you communicate with your partner, you develop a clearer sense of what's worth paying attention to and what issues are worth bringing up for discussion. If you bombard your partner with every single thing that annoys you about them, you're not focusing on the things that really matter. If you want to address something in your relationship in an impactful way, the key is to see what's open for negotiation. How do you know?

Any issue that has long-term consequences for your relationship is something you want to bring up with your partner. If it's an issue that's pushing your buttons over and over again, and/or if it's something that's going to help your partner grow, it's a good idea to address it. Issues related to time, dirt, and money often fall into this category.

Again, when you're communicating with your partner around these issues, you want to let go of the idea that you're right and the other person is wrong because they have a different perspective or experience. The more you can communicate with your partner from a place of love, hope, and good intentions, the more you get to communicate, and the more satisfying that communication feels as your relationship matures.

How to Communicate When You Don't Feel Valued

Sometimes you understand that your partner isn't trying to hurt you, but you can't help being triggered. In this case, if you express what's happening for you, it allows your partner to see the effect of their behavior on you—and gives them a chance to change it. Here are some examples:

> *"Hey, partner, when you come home from work and don't communicate with me, I start to feel that I'm not important to you. What's happening for you?"*

> *"Hey, partner, sometimes when you interrupt me, I get scared that you don't value what I think. My logical side knows it's irrational, but my emotional side doesn't. What's happening for you?"*

However, even if you're making an effort to communicate what's going on for you with understanding and love, it's important to keep in mind that your partner might not be on the same page. They might not respond right away—or they might act defensive. If that happens, what do you do?

Whenever you bring up an issue with your partner, it's important to let go of the expectation that they're going to respond the way you want them to. As I mentioned in chapter 10, it can be extremely difficult for the people we care about to hear how they've hurt us. Their negative minds automatically start to catastrophize, spiraling into thoughts like, "Hey, this relationship isn't as secure as I thought."

When you have that first conversation with your partner about something that's bothering you, it's important to keep in mind that you're opening the door to change. Your partner is going to register it on some level, but how much they register it will depend on how they were feeling and what was going on for them in that moment.

Depending on how big the issue is, you may have to have many more conversations about it going forward, as it's likely to come up in some other way. After all, it takes long enough for us to change something in ourselves. When we want our partners to change, too, it can take time for them to buy into the idea and embrace it.

At the same time, if you're communicating your issue with love, there's a good chance that your partner is listening and that they'll integrate your input at some point. The key is to keep your feedback short, sweet, and light. (Unless it's a big deal, you don't want your input to come across as heavy or relationship-threatening.) Then make an effort to be aware of how your partner is doing what you asked; this way, you reinforce their behavior and allow the change to grow. (Later in this chapter we'll go into more detail about the importance of acknowledging your partner when they change their behavior for you.)

However, if you take this loving, hopeful approach to communication over and over again and your partner doesn't respond—or if you think they're intentionally trying to hurt you—it might be time to reevaluate your relationship.

If you're feeling like something's missing in your relationship, ask for what you want from a positive place. For example, if you want more quality time with your partner, start with something like, "Remember that time we spent all day at the beach? I loved that. Can we pick a day to do that again?"

Wanting more sex is another example. Instead of pressuring your partner for more sex, do things that make them feel more attractive, more secure, more loved. Over time, your partner will feel inspired to have sex with you more often.

Paying attention to how your partner likes to get feedback can also help you create what you want in your relationship. For example, whereas I like to understand the larger picture around any feedback someone's giving me, my husband Mark wants to hear it in one sentence.

If I can't condense my input into twenty words, then it's more difficult for him to process what I'm saying. If I give him something digestible, easy, and quick, he usually responds in a positive way.

Besides paying attention to how your partner likes to receive input, be aware of your timing. Sometimes we're so anxious about sharing our perspective or getting our point across that we make the mistake of communicating something regardless of what's happening with our partner in that moment.

Before you bring up what's going on for you, pay attention to where your partner is. Are they on their way out the door? Are they tired? Have they just finished a long day at work? Are they relaxed? Just wanting to have fun? When you're trying to create more of what you want in your relationship, be strategic about choosing the right moment to talk with your partner.

PRACTICE

Think of one thing your partner does on an ongoing basis that annoys you or hurts your feelings. Now write down your emotions in relation to their behavior as you originally feel them. For example, "I'm upset because of X," or "You're wrong because of Y."

Now, holding on to the idea that your partner doesn't want to hurt you, and that they have good intentions for you, write down your emotions as you want to express them. For example, "I know you don't mean to do X, but it makes me feel Y." This is how you start to communicate your feelings with love and relate to your partner's behavior differently.

THE FOURTH INGREDIENT: ACKNOWLEDGE YOUR PARTNER WHEN THEY CHANGE TO MEET YOUR NEEDS

When your partner adjusts their behavior to meet your needs, it's important to recognize their effort. Just as you celebrate yourself with each baby step toward your goals, you want to recognize your partner every time they do something to take better care of you.

In my practice, I've met many couples who miss the opportunity to look for evidence that their partner is changing to meet their needs. "I did everything you said," some of them will tell me, "and they didn't change!" Since they've made such an effort to communicate their needs with love, they assume their partner will change right away, or they expect their partner to respond in a particular way. What happens then? More often than not, their partner feels inadequate for not being acknowledged for the changes they tried to make. Then they return to the status quo.

For example, let's say you want your partner to become a better listener. They're not going to go from being a terrible listener to an attentive one in a week. But maybe they'll listen more carefully to you at a certain moment or catch themselves before they interrupt you.

These baby steps are the things you want to be looking for and paying attention to. Instead of holding on the story in your head about your partner being a bad listener—and looking for evidence to support that story—you want to be aware of the moments when your partner is creating a new story. And you want to acknowledge those moments by saying something like, "Thank you for listening. That really made a difference to me and made me feel cared about."

It's much easier to sustain a healthy romantic relationship by focusing on what's going well instead of fixating on what's going wrong. Telling people what they're doing wrong doesn't usually change their behavior; in fact, it often motivates them to rebel against being told what to do. On the other hand, when you pay attention to the positive aspects of your relationship, you help grow them.

Instead of making them feel like they have to change or else, the goal is to inspire your partner to want to be with you. By celebrating your partner when they take a step in your direction—through verbal acknowledgment and/or physical affection—you motivate them to keep doing things that make you happy.

RELATIONSHIPS ARE WORK—TO A DEGREE

Despite everything I've been saying about how to sustain a healthy romantic relationship, I think it's confusing when people say relationships are work. In some sense they are: Your romantic relationships are the most emotionally volatile place in your life. Why? Your partner is usually the person you're most dedicated to. They're the person you spend the most time with. So it's inevitable that they're going to trigger you emotionally, especially when they do things that go against your established patterns or bring up unresolved issues from your childhood.

In this sense, relationships are hard work, because your emotional territory can be challenging to navigate. However, the more emotionally aware you are—and the more in touch you are with your attachment style and your established patterns from childhood—the easier it is to navigate that territory. In other words, once you get to the point where your relationship with yourself is strong, relationships aren't such hard work.

Or at least they shouldn't be, especially in the beginning. When clients come to me at the beginning of a relationship and tell me how much pain they're in, I tell them they may want to rethink things.

In your first year together, you should be happy eighty percent of the time. If you're crying, feeling bad about yourself, or putting in an enormous amount of energy into making it work, it can mean one of two things: either the person isn't right for you, or you're bringing your unresolved traumas into the relationship. It could also be a combination of both.

WHEN TO LET GO

How do you know when it's time to end a relationship? When you've done everything you can to bring the best version of yourself to it, and you still feel like something is missing, it could be time to let go.

This is what happened to Charlette, whose story opens this chapter. Eventually, she learned to stop depending on Liam to ease her depression. Little by little, as she started to fulfill her own needs and embrace her life, they grew closer again. But after a while, she felt a pit in her stomach.

"Something isn't right," she told me. "It just feels hard. I've worked through my issues, but when I'm with him, our dynamic doesn't inspire me to be the person I want to be."

Liam's attitude toward his depression was driving a wedge between them. Charlette was fighting hard to cope with her feelings of depression. Liam's viewpoint was more resigned: "We have depression in my family, and it is what it is," he told her. He took anti-depressants, and that was as far as he wanted to go to cope with his emotions. In other words, he thought of depression as part of his story. But Charlette didn't want it to be a part of hers anymore.

Eventually, Charlette broke up with Liam. In the end, they simply weren't right for each other.

Whether or not you believe in the idea of soul mates, the truth is that it's rare to find someone you can align with emotionally, sexually, and intellectually. On top of that, even if you find that person, sometimes you don't align when it comes to making life decisions in a partnership.

But that doesn't mean you should stop looking. It just means you might experience a few breakups before you find someone who's right for you.

In the dating world, everything else is a mismatch before you find someone you want to be with long-term. So when things don't work out in a relationship, it doesn't mean you're a loser or the other person is a jerk. It just means you don't happen to be a match.

In other words, when you break up with someone, it's important to remember that your value as a human being (and your ex's value as a human being) is completely separate from your relationship status.

If things fall apart, it's not because you're unlovable. It's because you're incompatible, you're at different places in your life, and you want different things. There's nothing wrong with you—or them—for the fact that you don't belong together.

KEEPING THE PASSION ALIVE

Once you do find someone you want to commit to, it can be a challenge to keep the passion alive over time. So how do you hold on to that sense of excitement and keep your relationship from turning dull?

If my relationship with Mark starts to feel stagnant, the first thing I do is ask myself what I'm giving to it. Why?

If I don't put one hundred percent of myself into being the best partner I can be, I can't expect to get one hundred percent back.

On one level, it's wonderful that we're raising our expectations of what we want from our partners. Yes, we deserve to be treated as equals. Yes, we want to feel empowered and supported. At the same time, though, it's important to ask ourselves if we're giving what we're asking for.

How does this look in practice? With Mark, I think about what he might need and how I could do a better job giving it to him. This could be anything from picking up my clothes from the bedroom floor to spicing up our sex life to acknowledging what I love about him.

When I make a conscious effort to be more loving and giving, Mark always responds by taking better care of me. I don't have to say anything. It happens naturally.

KEEP YOUR PASSION FOR YOURSELF ALIVE

Besides asking yourself how to be a better partner, it's important to continue creating your own passion and excitement as your relationship matures.

In other words, if you want to keep the passion alive, practice returning again and again to the first ingredient in the recipe for a successful relationship: fulfilling your own needs. As you grow closer to your partner, you want to continue growing closer to yourself.

When you keep your life interesting and continue doing things that make you feel alive, you put yourself in a space of self-love. When you're in that space, you don't need your partner to take care of you all the time. But when you do need taking care of, they feel inspired to do it, and it makes them feel good.

Even if something pulls you away from that space, no matter what's happening in your relationship, once you've experienced the feeling of self-love, you can always come back to it. Always.

PRACTICE

What are three things you can do to be a better partner right now? If you can't answer that question, then ask your partner what they need from you.

Once you zero in on what you can be doing better in your relationship, start by making a month-long plan. Pick one thing that feels easy. Observe how doing that thing feels for you and how your partner responds.

For example, if you want to make your partner feel more desired, initiate sex. If you want to be more romantic, plan dates and/or change out of your sweat pants when you're hanging around the house. If you want to be more supportive, run errands for your partner or think about other ways you could make their life easier. If you want to be more open about your feelings, tell them what you're grateful for and what you love about them.

When that first month is over, reflect on how your actions impacted your relationship. Take a few minutes to write about it. The next month, choose the same activity or pick something else to focus on that feels doable and fun.

In the end, everything we do brings our partners closer to us or pushes them away. If you're making a conscious effort to be a better partner, you not only create the possibility to be more intimate with your partner—you also empower yourself to feel more fulfilled in the relationship.

CONCLUSION

LAUNCHING YOUR LIFE

For my client Chloe, whose story opens this book, deciding to become the best version of herself was one thing. It was quite another thing for her to keep following through with that decision.

When she stopped using alcohol to numb her anxiety, she came face to face with the pain of her past. The more she explored her emotional history—growing up as the child of divorced parents and having a tumultuous relationship with her mom—the harder it became to cope with the voices in her negative mind.

"This isn't working at all," she told me. "I feel way worse than when I started. I'm having more self-hating thoughts than I've ever had."

What Chloe was going through is what we all experience when we're on the cusp of making major changes in our lives: The closer she came to changing her story, the more her negative mind resisted that change.

Over time, as she learned to recognize, and eventually lower, the voice of her negative mind, Chloe's vision for her life started to expand. After giving up alcohol, she changed her diet, cutting out junk food little by little until she ultimately decided to go vegan. As she felt better in her body, her head started to clear. After years of searching for a professional direction, she finally figured out what she was interested in: marketing and branding. Despite her lack of experience, she got a prestigious marketing job at a successful startup.

But her struggles didn't end there. Once she learned to cope with her inner resistance, Chloe ran into resistance from another source: some of her family and friends. Though many of the people in her life accepted and encouraged her transformation, a few of them felt threatened by it.

"Who are you?" they said. "You don't even look like the same person."

In other words, who did she think she was, making all these changes to her life? It was hard enough for Chloe to hold on to everything that was new in her life. Now she had to deal with the prospect of losing part of her support system, too.

What could she do? The first step was to recognize that their behavior wasn't rooted in bad intentions. It was actually an expression of fear. As Chloe learned to love herself, the people close to her could feel her changing. However, instead of expressing their fear of losing her, they unconsciously resisted the change because they didn't know how to relate to her yet.

Chloe's story is the story of how we grow. Every time you

take a step forward, something pushes you back. Every time you reach a new level of awareness or fulfillment, you can expect to face resistance, either from yourself or the people close to you. This is how you develop the resilience to integrate the changes you make in your life.

Ultimately, Chloe learned to reframe the resistance she faced as she transformed herself. The more she changed, the easier it was to understand why her family and friends felt threatened. But she didn't let that stop her from moving forward.

Every time she got knocked off her path, Chloe found her way back to it. While she was working toward her bachelor's degree in marketing, she landed a coveted internship with a major winemaker, where they offered her a job after she graduated. Besides rewriting her past relationships, she's learned to create new ones. She surrounds herself with people who reflect the love she feels for herself.

Are Chloe's challenges over? Of course they aren't. But no matter what happens in her life, her connection with her true self will always be there. Even if she loses it, she knows how to repair it.

HOW TO CONNECT TO YOUR TRUE SELF

For Chloe, and for all of us, the process of connecting with our true self starts with accepting and learning to cope with our emotions. When it comes to anxiety, anger, and depression, the same idea applies: What you resist will persist, and what you accept will transform.

ANXIETY

We all feel anxious to some degree. However, we get stuck in anxiety by not allowing ourselves to feel our fear. So how do you let go of anxiety? The key is to allow yourself to feel your fear instead of judging yourself for feeling it. After that, the next step is to understand that all anxiety is rooted in the future—never in the present. Unless a bear is attacking you right now, the anxiety you're feeling is about something you *think* might happen. So come back to the moment.

ANGER

Unlike anxiety, anger is a secondary emotion. It's a defense against fear and sadness. When we're angry, we sometimes think we're in a powerful place, but it's not true. Like a dog growling in a corner, we use anger as a defense to create distance to keep from getting hurt. To unravel anger, you have to go underneath it and find the fear. What is anger trying to tell you? Once you figure out your root fear, you can ease it either by addressing it internally or by communicating your feelings in a state of calm.

DEPRESSION

Despite what our culture tells us about depression being a disease or an inherited condition, it's actually a problem that can be fixed. Similar to anxiety, depression comes from swallowing your feelings and judging yourself for feeling them. Easing depression starts with accepting your feelings—whatever they are—and allowing them to move through you. When you let yourself feel sad, or scared, or angry, you not only lower the intensity of negative emotions. You also keep them from stacking up and becoming stagnant in your body.

CALMING THE MIND

Anxiety, anger, and depression are all rooted in the way our minds work. Though most of us no longer live in the wilderness and don't have to worry about our minute-to-minute survival, our minds haven't evolved beyond that time. In other words, our minds are biologically programmed to keep us alive by making sure we remain in a hyper-vigilant state. They aren't designed to keep us happy and at peace.

So how do you calm the negative mind? By admitting that it's there. Once you acknowledge the negative mind, you can turn down the volume in two ways: 1) being aware of when it's taken over 2) learning to separate the negative mind voice from the voice of your true self. Though meditation is the easiest way to practice calming the negative mind, it's definitely not the only way. Doing things you love, things that make you feel inspired and joyful, is another way. The important thing is to experiment until you find a method(s) that works for you—and practice it consistently.

THE IMPORTANCE OF THE BODY

Taking care of your physical body is one of the keys to changing your relationship with your emotions. Though most of us are intellectually aware of the mind-body connection, we underestimate the power of diet and exercise when it comes to how we feel.

Besides diet and exercise, your relationship with alcohol and drugs also has a huge impact on your emotional health. When you're evaluating this relationship, the key is not to judge it. Instead, look at whether the substances in your life lead to negative consequences—and to what degree.

The easiest way to make this assessment is to give up a particular substance entirely for a period of time. Unless you completely disconnect from alcohol and drugs for a while, you can't redo your relationship with them.

FINDING YOUR DIRECTION

When you develop healthier ways to cope with your emotions, and a more conscious relationship with your body, it's easier to see where you want to take your life—and connect your goals with your true self.

The key to finding your direction is to pick one. Say you have ten strengths and you find a job that utilizes three or four of them—go for it! Then try to find the meaning in it. No matter what the work is, don't do it passively. Don't approach it as a means to an end. Be in it fully. The more you can find the meaning in your work, the more clearly you can see what your potential is, where you want to go next, and what careers could be fulfilling for you.

YOUR RELATIONSHIP WITH MONEY

As you transition into career and adulthood, it's important to handle your relationship with money like any other emotional process in your life. Like all relationships, it's rooted in your childhood.

Once you evaluate your history with money, you can decide how you want to relate to it now—and create goals around it. If your money goal is only about a number, it won't make you happy, even after you reach it. The key to achieving your money goals is to connect them with your true self, to something that inspires you in your core.

FALLING IN LOVE WITH YOURSELF

Strengthening your emotional coping mechanisms, caring for your physical self, finding your direction, and developing a healthy relationship with money are all preparation for the process of falling in love with yourself. The more you learn to practice self-love, the more you can connect with others and create the relationships you want.

When it comes to creating healthy relationships, you need to look back before you move forward. Evaluating your emotional history and your relationship with your parents/caregivers reduces your risk of carrying false beliefs and unconscious patterns into your adult relationships.

At the same time, it's important to remember that we all have imperfect parents/caregivers (who were also raised by imperfect parents). When you can humanize and accept the people who raised you, you set yourself up for satisfying friendships and healthy romantic relationships throughout your life.

As you process pain from childhood, friendships can be a crucial source of support. They're also an important training ground for healthy communication in your other, more charged relationships. The beauty of friendship is that your friends don't need to fulfill all your needs; you can have as many friends as you want. As a place of total acceptance, friendships also help you develop your feelings of self-love.

Before you can fall in love with someone else, you need to fall in love with yourself first. How does that work? Turn off the dating apps and try dating yourself for six months to a year. Make a list of your strengths and read through it every day. Explore your passions and go after your goals. Take care of your body. Stay connected to your friends. Experiment with activities that help you connect with your true self. Once you discover the beauty of your life, you're ready to share it with someone else.

However, when you finally find someone who inspires you to commit, it can be tempting to let go of yourself. The key to sustaining a healthy romantic relationship is to hold on to your love for yourself—and continue to deepen your passion for your own life. At the same time, you want to be conscious about being the best partner you can be.

CHOOSING THE PATH TO YOUR TRUE SELF

Whether it's changing your relationship with your emotions, your body, your career, your finances, and/or the people in your life, the process of transformation starts with taking baby steps.

What step can you take right now to move in a positive direction? As you work toward becoming the best version of yourself, keep asking yourself this question.

Remember, the size and quality of the step don't matter. What matters is that you take it—and celebrate yourself afterward.

The way to happiness and fulfillment starts with acknowledging every success, no matter how small it seems. The more you celebrate yourself during the journey, the easier it is to keep going until you're living the life you want.

Becoming the best version of yourself is about choosing the path to your true self—over and over again. You have the power to launch your life. Where do you want to start?

APPENDIX

EMDR: AN ALTERNATIVE FOR TRAPPED EMOTIONS

While I don't believe in quick fixes for chronic psychological problems like anxiety and depression, Eye Movement Desensitization and Reprocessing (EMDR) therapy can be an effective way to access and release stagnated emotions. If you've tried other forms of therapy and they haven't worked for you, EMDR offers a potential solution.

HOW DOES EMDR WORK?

EMDR connects both hemispheres of the brain through rapid eye movements (moving your eyes back and forth), alternating sounds (listening through headphones to beeping sounds on one side, then the other), or body tapping (tapping your knees or shoulders one after the other).

When you go through something traumatic or feel any type of intense emotion, your right brain absorbs that experience. Afterward, when you're trying to work through the experience, you use the left side of the brain, which controls language.

When you use movement, sound, or touch to connect both the right and left sides of the brain simultaneously, it allows you to reprocess the trauma and release it in a different way.

WHO CAN BENEFIT FROM EMDR?

Therapists initially developed EMDR to treat war veterans, rape victims, and other victims of extreme trauma. However, therapists have expanded the treatment to help people deal with feelings of pain, anger, or social anxiety, as well as people with chronic psychological problems like anxiety. It's also been effective for people who can't let go of their negative beliefs about themselves, such as thinking they're not lovable.

Basically, EMDR is an alternative for anyone who feels trapped in a negative emotional loop and wants to free themselves from their pain.

EMDR ALONE ISN'T ENOUGH

Though EMDR can be an effective way to release stagnated emotions, it's important to use it in conjunction with something else, especially if you're dealing with chronic psychological problems. In other words, EMDR can serve as a supplement to the emotional work you're already doing, but it's not going to heal you on its own.

GETTING STARTED WITH EMDR

If you want to use EMDR to change negative beliefs about yourself, you can actually learn to perform it on yourself. Laurel Parnell's *Tapping In: A Step-by-Step Guide to Activating Your Healing Resources Through Bilateral Stimulation* is an excellent beginners' guide. The book provides step-by-step instructions and easy-to-learn exercises to help you heal yourself through bilateral stimulation.

However, if you're looking to EMDR as a treatment for trauma, it's important to work with a licensed therapist. The EMDR International Association (emdria.org) has a directory of EMDR therapists around the world. Since it's designed to help you release specific experiences, EMDR is not an ongoing treatment; it usually requires just a few sessions.

In the meantime, if you'd like to get a clearer picture of what can potentially happen during an EMDR session, check out episode four of my podcast, where I share some of my own experiences with EMDR: http://www.jesse-giunta-rafeh. com/podcast/2019/1/28/episode-4-emdr

REFERENCES AND RECOMMENDED READING

Allen Carr, *Allen Carr's Easy Way to Stop Smoking* (London: Penguin, 2015): Carr goes through our most common deeply held beliefs about smoking and then unravels them. If you want to quit smoking or vaping, this is one of the best resources out there.

Malcolm Gladwell, *Blink: The Power of Thinking Without Thinking* (New York: Little, Brown and Company, 2005): Gladwell explores how we make hundreds of unconscious decisions in the blink of an eye—and how our initial judgments can sometimes cloud our perception of other people. If you're working on releasing judgment and being more open, his ideas are especially helpful.

John M. Gottman and Nan Silver, *The Seven Principles for Making Marriage Work: A Practical Guide from the Country's Foremost Relationship Expert* (New York: Three Rivers Press,

1999): Dr. Gottman spent over twenty years researching the factors that go into a healthy marriage. His book
focuses on the seven key ingredients of a harmonious,
long-lasting relationship. He also includes questionnaires
and practical exercises to help your relationship reach its
highest potential.

Darren Hardy, *The Compound Effect* (New York: Vanguard
Press, 2010): Hardy explores how the small, everyday decisions we make over time can add up to big changes in our
lives. He breaks down the idea of taking baby steps toward
your goals.

Robert T. Kiyosaki, *Rich Dad Poor Dad: What the Rich Teach
Their Kids About Money That the Poor and Middle Class Do
Not!* (New York: Warner Books Edition, 1997): This is
Kiyosaki's story about growing up with two fathers: his
biological father and his best friend's father. He learned
powerful lessons from both men, including the idea that
you don't need to earn a high income to create wealth. One
of the best-selling personal finance books of all time.

Amir Levine and Rachel Heller, *Attached: The New Science of
Adult Attachment and How It Can Help You Find—and Keep—
Love* (New York: TarcherPerigee, 2010): Understanding the
nature of adult attachment can help us create and sustain
healthy romantic relationships. This book explores the science behind the three primary attachment styles—anxious,
avoidant, and secure—and guides you toward determining
your own attachment style, which helps you build more fulfilling connections with the people you love.

Mark Manson, *The Subtle Art of Not Giving a F*ck: A Coun-*

terintuitive Approach to Living a Good Life (New York: HarperCollins, 2016): A great resource if you're struggling to find your professional direction. Manson debunks the idea that you have to find your passion before you can choose a career. He also questions the common belief that we have to be extraordinary in order to feel happy and fulfilled.

Jane McGonigal, *SuperBetter: The Power of Living Gamefully* (New York: Penguin Books, 2015): McGonigal cites multiple scientific studies to show how games increase physical, mental, and emotional strength. She also provides a series of simple, meditation-simulating activities to help improve the mind's resilience and ease anxiety.

Laurel Parnell Ph.D., *Tapping In: A Step-by-Step Guide to Activating Your Healing Resources Through Bilateral Stimulation* (Boulder: Sounds True Inc., 2008): A self-guided program for learning Eye Movement Desensitization and Reprocessing (EMDR), a form of therapy that can help heal trauma, boost confidence, calm the body, and relieve stress. A potential alternative for releasing trapped emotions, especially when other forms of therapy haven't been effective.

Guy Raz, *How I Built This with Guy Raz* (podcast), National Public Radio, https://www.npr.org/podcasts/510313/how-i-built-this: Host Guy Raz talks to entrepreneurs, innovators, and idealists about the process of bringing their visions to life. A great resource for learning about the stories behind some of the most powerful companies in the world—and getting inspired about your own visions.

Geneen Roth, *Women, Food and God: An Unexpected Path to*

Almost Everything (London: Simon & Schuster Ltd., 2011): Roth draws on her own experience and struggles around eating and weight gain to help us rethink the role of food in our lives. A fantastic resource if you're looking to change your relationship with food for the better.

Matthew Ferry, Thack Nguyen, Marc Sachnoff, and Kristen Marie Scheuerlein, *The Gift: A Revolution in Networking Mastery* (USA: Global Rakkaus Press, 2011): If the idea of networking makes you nervous, this book will help you get out there and do it. Not only does it make networking less scary, but it also gives it a purpose.

Bessel van der Kolk M.D., *The Body Keeps the Score: Brain, Mind, and Body in the Healing of Trauma* (New York: Penguin Books, 2014): In over thirty years of working with survivors of trauma, Dr. van der Kolk observed how trauma actually reshapes the body and brain. He explores a variety of treatments—including biofeedback, meditation, sports, drama, and yoga—to help people recover by activating the brain's natural capacity to heal.

ACKNOWLEDGMENTS

Toni, you held my hand through every important step I took in my twenties. You've made the biggest impact in my life in terms of how I help my clients and see the world of psychology. I've learned as much from your teachings as from the person you are: spunky, heart-driven, and creative. Without you, I wouldn't be the therapist or the person I am.

Mark, you are my rock, my laughter, my advisor, and most importantly, my soul mate. Being with you pushes me to reach higher and to look at the world as a place of endless possibilities. You live and think beyond conventional limits, and you've taught me to do the same. I feel eternally grateful for what you bring into my life.

Mom, you are my role model, my support, and one of my best friends. I love the way we continue to grow and learn together. Thank you for seeing me, for laughing with me, and for crying with me. Thank you for making me feel like I can do anything—and, at the same time, for reminding me that I'm enough, just as I am.

Dad, you taught me some of the most important life lessons: how to look at people from an empathetic perspective, how to become the most productive version of myself, and how to focus on what truly matters in this life. When I went to college I was surprised at how often I found myself quoting you. I still do.

Jill, you've supported me in every way imaginable, from editing blogs to creating the podcast to listening to me talk through all my doubts and fears. I value your presence, your support, and your opinion more than you know. I'm so grateful that you've been a part of my journey.

Layne, you were my partner in creating this book. Your thousands of questions, your genuine curiosity to understand what I'm teaching, your drive to get it right, and your talent made this book what it is. I could not have asked for a better partner. Not only did we get it right, but it was also a fulfilling adventure to work with you along the way.

Matthew and Kristen, you introduced me to the world of the spirit. Though I rebelled against it for a long time, the way you presented spirituality—and embodied it—forever changed my life. I saw the world differently after my first meditation workshop with you. Since then, your perspective and your presence in my life have continued to help me find a deeper state of peace. Your teachings are all over this book because they are now a part of me.

Sarah, thank you for being my biggest cheerleader. Thank you for giving me the confidence to tap into my power. I love your vulnerability, your positivity, and the energy you bring with you wherever you go. You inspire me.

Zoë, my wise soul sister, I'm so grateful to be on this journey with you, and to have known you all these years. I love the depth of our connection. I love that the time we spend together never feels like enough. I love the way you push me to grow. I love that we always seem to have a blast, no matter what we're doing. Life feels sweet and fulfilling with you in it.

Jennifer, you're the eyes behind making my dreams come true. Not only do you make me feel completely supported, understood, and taken care of, but you're also an extremely talented artist who understands my ideas and brings them to life. Thank you for making all the uncomfortable parts of this journey (like taking my author photo and designing the cover) fun. I love laughing with you, collaborating with you, and just spending time with you.

My clients, I'm more grateful to you than you might realize. You are what excites me about going to work every day. You inspired me to write this book. There is nothing on this planet more fulfilling to me than seeing you create the lives that you want to live! Thank you for trusting me with the deepest parts of you, and for allowing me to be a part of your journeys.

ABOUT THE AUTHOR

JESSE GIUNTA RAFEH is a psychotherapist and certified success coach who's helped hundreds of young adults who feel lost find clarity and direction in their lives. As a teenager, she struggled with anxiety, depression, and chronic self-doubt. Through her own emotional journey, she developed the tools and methodology that have helped her empower her clients. Jesse's primary motivation and deepest satisfaction lies in the transformation she sees her clients achieve—through their own dedication, self-discovery, and strength.

Jesse lives in California with her husband, Mark. To learn more about Jesse's work, visit jesse-giunta-rafeh.com.